ELIAS VORPAHL
The Word Trove

Translated from the German by
Romy Fursland

ELIAS VORPAHL

THE WORD TROVE

1st edition January 2021
© 2021 Iron Bird Publishing, Munich
© 2021 Sebastian Vogel, Munich
All rights reserved
Translated from the German by Romy Fursland, Norwich
Illustrations by Julia Marie Stolba, Munich
Cover design by Lena Toschka, Leipzig
Cover illustration by Julia Marie Stolba, Munich
Layout and typesetting by Lena Toschka, Leipzig
Typeface: Sabon
Printed and bound by GGP Media GmbH, Pößneck
Printed in Germany
ISBN 978-3-00-066543-1

www.thewordtrove.com

For in the end,
all we are doing is seeking
to weave poetry into life,
to find poetry in life itself.

Taken from a letter written by Michael Ende
to his friend Peter Boccarius, dated 24 June 1949

FOR DIANA

PROLOGUE

The old man took up his quill. Now he knew how the story should begin. How he'd despaired, aware of how fleeting his discovery was! His mind had been full of so many details, but he hadn't been able to stitch them all together. Something vital had been missing. But today, he knew what to do. He paced up and down the little hut one last time, glancing at the sheets of paper covered in scribbled notes. This time, he didn't simply add to them. Instead, he sat down at his desk, dipped his quill in the inkpot and wrote: 'The old man took up his quill …'

CHAPTER
ONE

Speechlessness

The Word woke up. The little letter on its right syllable had gone completely numb. It threw off its blanket and stretched its syllables until all the weariness had gone out of them. Then it got up slowly, dressed, yawned and went into the kitchen, where its parents had laid the table for breakfast.

Its father lowered his newspaper. "While you've been sleeping the day away, the world's got a darned sight crazier," he announced.

The Word skirted around the table and gave its mother a kiss. "Why?" it asked. "What's happened?"

"They've increased the defence budget again. If things carry on like this, all our research at the Institute will soon just be about finding ways to protect wordkind from humanity. It's absurd!"

"So there are ways?" said the Word, biting off a mouthful of toast.

"Of protecting ourselves, you mean?" Its father sized it up from left to right. His child's wordlets had touched a nerve. "We words don't need to protect ourselves. What we really need to be doing is thinking about how to get more humans to read and write. Writing embodies us in our purest form, in absolute clarity. But when we're spoken, we get lost in meaninglessness. That's where the real danger lies."

"Daaad, please!" The Word rolled its eyes.

"Let's change the subject," its mother chimed in. "Have you seen who's going to be hosting the Linguistic Games this year?"

"No. But let me finish, it's important. If humans stop reading us, we'll be forgotten. Words will disappear, and our world will cease to exist."

"Dad, no one *seriously* believes that words need humans.

You're the only one who thinks that. Have you ever heard of a word just disappearing off the face of the earth? No: all you ever hear about are terrible stories in the newspapers about words who've been spoken out loud, getting mangled and garbled and deformed. Why would anyone believe you?"

"The Linguistics are going to be hosted by Wordsmith again this year," offered the Word's mother once more – but nobody was listening.

"It's not about belief," said the Word's father. "It's about facts, proven by research. We can't just demonise human beings. We need them; they read and write us. They enable us to exist. Without them, our world would disappear much more quickly than we think."

"Enough! I've had enough of this! Everything's always about you and your research! Have you ever once thought about us? You built our whole house to look like a giant book, just to get your message across to the rest of the world! Do you know how ridiculous that is? How ridiculous all my friends think it is?" The Word jumped up from the table.

"I thought you liked this house! Come along now, don't get your vowels in a twist. Sit down and we can talk about this."

"No!" the Word retorted. It left its parents at the breakfast table and stormed out of the house.

Why did Dad always have to be so stubborn about his research? The house wasn't the issue at all. It was a lovely house, and the Word couldn't care less what anyone else said or thought. It was just annoying the way Dad was always so convinced of his own opinion.

The Word followed the wide road that led to his friend

Deaf's house. Other words would probably have been overawed by the sheer size of the house, but the Word had known Deaf since they were very young, and it strode confidently through the open gate. The servants spotted the Word as it approached the front door, and immediately busied themselves with preparations to welcome their master's guest. They arranged themselves in two long rows outside the double doors of the Great Hall. The Word greeted some of the servants whom it knew by sight. But despite being friends with Deaf for so long, it still didn't know all their names – there were just too many of them. The Word entered the Great Hall, which was Deaf's favourite room because it was the most spacious. The servants filed in behind it in a long line and formed a large circle around the room, standing one behind the other. The words which Deaf tended to use most often stood right at the front. In the centre of the hall was a podium, and on it a leather armchair. Deaf sat in the chair and prepared for their conversation by doing stretching exercises with his fingers. When the Word reached the podium, Deaf pointed to a word in the front row of the circle of servants. The word called out its own name:

"I!"

Then Deaf pointed to another word. This too shouted its name: "Was!"

Deaf swivelled in his chair and pointed to another word standing in the circle right behind him.

"Hoping ..."

And so it went on: Deaf pointed to eight of his servants in turn, and they all announced their names one after the other to form a sentence: "I was hoping you would drop by again."

"It is great to see you," said the Word.

Deaf spun around in his chair, surveying the whole of the circle. His servants stepped out of the circle in a certain order – first the word *It*, then the word *Is*, and finally the word *You*.

Deaf watched the words as they presented themselves. He knew all their names, and nodded in understanding. The Word went up to the podium and embraced his friend.

The Word proceeded to tell him what had just happened at home. Deaf was a good listener. He swivelled on his armchair, watching attentively and taking note of each word as it stepped forward. When the Word had finished speaking, Deaf pointed to his servants one by one to compose sentences:

"Your dad is always the same."

The words called out their names.

"It is such a contradiction," Deaf went on. "The rest of the world tries to stay as far away as possible from humans, and yet your dad insists we cannot do without them. How can that be?"

"I know. And even if it's true, and we do need humans, how can we ever win them over? And how can we protect ourselves against them?"

The word *Protect* was standing quite a long way back, so it took a while for it to come all the way to the front.

Deaf replied: "I can't tell you how to win them over." The word *I* was out of breath from all the leaping around and shouting it was having to do. "But I can tell you a few ways to keep humans at bay."

"How?" asked the Word.

Its dad had often talked of the dangers of being spoken out loud, and the importance of being read by a human being. But he'd never said anything about how that worked in practice. He was a researcher, and had devoted his life to studying theoretical matters.

Deaf looked at his friend for a moment, then started to swivel on his chair again, composing more sentences.

"When I was younger, for a long time I wanted to be somebody else. This hall did not exist then, and I had no servants. I was a young word who could neither hear nor speak."

The Word already knew the story. Deaf came from a very rich family, but one who didn't make a show of their wealth. The family had built this huge mansion solely for their deaf child, so that there would be enough room for all the word-servants. Ever since he was little, Deaf had had to learn to form words in his own special way. But many words found it too complicated and laborious to communicate like this, which meant Deaf didn't have many friends he could talk to. The Word, on the other hand, was not bothered by Deaf's unusual way of speaking. It had always loved puzzles and brainteasers, and when it had met Deaf, their first few conversations had felt a little bit like that.

"What are you getting at?" asked the Word.

"When I was younger, I often wished I could just fade away, become transparent to the world and the words in it. I tried every possible combination to achieve this, until one day I finally succeeded."

"Succeeded in what?"

"I rearranged myself."

"Rearranged yourself?" the Word echoed.

"Yes. If you want to protect yourself against humans, you need to be rare – you need to become a word that is seldom used. A foreign word, perhaps. Become cumbersome. Become a word that people do not use because nobody understands it. Become ugly: become an off-putting word."

Deaf had worked himself up into a frenzy. He pointed around the room in every direction. More and more words from the second and third rows called out their names, and when even that was not enough, more servants were called into the hall. It was hot and crowded. Only by standing high up on the podium could Deaf single out the words he needed.

"Every word has to find its own way to protect itself. If you become complicated, they will only use you rarely. Try to be difficult, unpronounceable, a tongue-twister. Then humans will fear you, instead of you fearing them. Change yourself, rearrange yourself, become something different!"

The Word stared blankly at its friend. "But how does that work, Deaf? How can I rearrange myself?"

At that moment something happened, something nobody could have expected – not the Word, not Deaf, and certainly not the hundreds of servants who were now crammed into the hall. It was Deaf who turned, fear dawning in his eyes, and suddenly pointed not at the servants but at the entrance to the hall. Two creatures were standing there, slender and straight-backed. None of the words in the room had ever seen them before, but they'd heard the stories and they all knew exactly what those creatures were. Vocal cords.

The cords stood motionless. Deaf wanted to say something, but there wasn't a single word he could call upon. Everyone in the hall was staring at the cords, poised erect in the doorway.

Then panic broke out. The words were so tightly packed together that they started to jostle each other. Those closest to the door surged backwards to escape the cords. Some of the words cried out. A few had fallen over and were desperately trying to get up again.

In the midst of all this chaos, the cords began to move. They contracted, stretched, contracted and stretched again. Then came the suction. Words were swept off their feet and skidded across the floor towards the opening that had appeared between the cords.

The first word – Deaf recognised *It* – was about to slip between the cords. The little word could not resist the suction, and neither could the others. More and more words began to disappear until whole clusters of them went tumbling into the chasm between the cords.

The armchair toppled and fell off the podium, and Deaf landed with a thud on the floor beside the Word. The force of the suction drew them both towards the cords. The Word tried to resist and hold on, but there was nothing to hold on to. Deaf clung to the podium with one hand, and grabbed his friend's wrist with the other. For a moment, they were able to resist the suction's pull.

There were hardly any words left in the hall now. Deaf looked into his friend's eyes, tears streaming down his face.

They had no way of speaking to each other anymore, but they didn't need to – they understood each other perfectly. The Word had tears in its eyes too. Then Deaf's strength failed him. His grip on the Word loosened, and it was swept away by the suction. Horrified, Deaf saw his friend being swallowed up by the vocal cords. A moment later, he let go of the armchair himself and went hurtling towards the cords.

The suction had stopped and the cords had vanished. It was quiet. Deaf lay curled up on the cold floor of the empty hall. It had been a long time since Deaf had felt so out of place. In fact, the word lying there on the floor of the hall was not Deaf anymore at all. Deaf hadn't had time to explain to his friend how words could rearrange themselves. His friend had disappeared, spoken out loud by a human being. But Deaf had managed to save himself. Just as he was being sucked towards the vocal cords, he'd rearranged himself. Deaf had become *Fade*. The suction had stopped, and the vocal cords had vanished. They'd overlooked him – just as he'd been overlooked as a child once he'd finally figured out how to rearrange himself.

It had been wonderful back then, at first. After rearranging himself to Fade for the very first time, he'd found he could hear and speak just like other words. He could finally do without his servants and leave his parents' mansion without losing the ability to communicate. It was all he'd ever wished for. But the more time he'd spent as Fade, the less at home he'd felt in this new world that had opened up to him. Other words took centre stage here, had opinions, shared ideas. He, meanwhile, stood on the sidelines and felt ignored. He knew what it meant to be Deaf; but what did it mean to be Fade? He'd fallen silent once more – not because he couldn't speak, but because he increasingly felt that what he had to say didn't matter.

Realisation had gradually dawned on him: just because he hadn't been able to speak like the other words didn't mean he'd actually wanted to *be* someone else. As Deaf, he hadn't had many friends, but the few he'd had – they really had *heard* him, he felt, in spite of his speechlessness. It was then that he'd decided never to rearrange himself again. It was his destiny to be a mute word, and he would accept his destiny. But then the vocal cords had come along, and now here he was. He'd been forced to become Fade, yet again.

He thought about all this as he lay there crying on the cold floor of the hall. He thought about all that he had lost – his servants, his unique way of communicating with other words ... and worst of all, his best friend, whom he had been unable to protect.

CHAPTER
TWO

Beginning & End

Warm and cold winds kept blowing in the Word's face from opposite directions, alternating every few seconds. Warm. Cold. Warm. Cold.

A foul smell was hanging in the dark air. The Word felt tight cords cutting into its syllables. It couldn't feel the ground beneath it, and seemed to be suspended in mid-air. Warm. Cold. Warm. Cold. It heard, very clearly, the voices of other words. Wherever it was, the Word was not alone.

"Out! Out! Let me out!" it heard.

Then, from a different direction, "What's going on?"

"Be quiet!" another word called out.

"Quiet? Quiet?!" asked another.

The Word tried to move, but the cords immediately tightened around its syllables.

"Argh!" it exclaimed.

"Don't struggle. There's nothing we can do," said a word from beside it.

The Word held still, and the straps loosened a little.

"You'll see for yourself in a second."

Then light came flooding in. Instinctively, the Word screwed up its eyes, but opened them again a moment later, curious to see where it was. It looked up to see a shaft crisscrossed by a web of knotted cords, in which various words were suspended. Here and there, the Word recognised some of Deaf's servants. *Can* was hanging from a cord nearby, and close to it was an indecisive-looking word called *Perhaps*. The Word itself was encircled by two long cords. They felt moist against its skin.

"The cords are going to catapult us up there," the word next to it said. He had worked for Deaf too, the Word was sure of it. What was his name again …?

"*H... H... Hint!*" The name came back to it.

"You've got a good memory," said Hint. Then he added, with urgency in his voice: "Now listen. You won't have much time. You're going to get catapulted up there, and when it happens you have to take a deep breath, as deep as you can. Remember, there's no point putting up a fight." The light disappeared again, and the shaft was plunged into darkness once more. "Oh and try not to listen to the screams. You have to block them out."

"What's going to happen to me up there?" asked the Word in terror, as the two cords suddenly started to tighten around its syllables again.

"You're about to be spoken!" it heard Hint say.

Then the cords that had been wrapped around the Word gave a sudden jolt. For a moment it flew upwards through the air towards the top of the shaft. It forced itself to take a deep breath. Then it crashed into a pool of liquid, hitting the surface so hard that all the breath was knocked out of it. The Word spluttered and flailed frantically, trying to stay afloat in the viscous liquid, but to no avail. The liquid was making its letters heavy and numb. The Word sank like a stone, fighting for every little bit of oxygen it could get. When the Word reached the bottom of the pool, the ground began to quake beneath its feet and the liquid ebbed away.

The Word gasped for breath. It lay exhausted on the rough, furry ground, which was gently vibrating. Cautiously, the Word opened its eyes, still gluey from the liquid. It blinked a few times until it could see more clearly. A cold wind was blowing in its face from the opening that lay ahead of it. Beyond the opening was a sheer drop. A handful of words lay between the Word and the abyss. One of them, sprawled on the ground, right next to the edge, was almost unrecognisable. *It* was covered in scratches and bruises, its mouth glued shut, its eyeballs sunk deep in their sockets. The short word's breathing was shallow.

After that, everything happened very fast. The rough ground beneath them shunted the words closer to the edge of the abyss, abruptly drew back and gave It a quick, sharp shove in the back.

"IIIIIIT!" The cry resounded through the space, earsplittingly loud. It echoed off the walls, making it even louder. It was a deep, pure cry that came from the word's very being. Forced out by a human, It had shouted itself.

It had disappeared, and it wasn't long before two more words followed suit, yelling out their names as they went. The Word tried not to listen to their screams, but in vain. A chill ran down its syllables. So this was how humans spoke. They tortured words. Dad was wrong, it thought. Humans are monsters!

The Word was next in line now, lying right in front of the opening. At that moment, it promised itself that it would never rely on being written or read by a human being. Suddenly it felt a blow to the back and, in agony, cried out the name it had carried within itself since its birth. Everything went dark. The world was swallowed up as if submerged in the blackest of ink.

When the Word awoke, the world was still enveloped in inky blackness. But the darkness wasn't as thick as it had been in the depths of the Word's unconsciousness. Now the obscurity was pierced by a flickering reddish-yellow light, and there was a crackling, rustling sound. The ground the Word was lying on felt soft. It wanted to turn towards the sound, but it was too weak. Its whole body ached.

"No, lie still." An old word's face appeared, bending over the Word. A woman. "You rest now, don't try to move," she whispered.

"Look after it, but don't exaggerate." It was a man's voice this time, but the Word couldn't see his face for it had already closed its eyes again.

"I have everything we need here," said the woman. "Cold compresses for the bruised letters, bandages for the cuts and some woundwort herb for the pain …"

Then the Word fell fast asleep.

When it awoke the next morning, an old man was sitting in a chair opposite it. He was stroking his grey beard with his index finger and thumb, staring into space, apparently lost in thought.

"Good morning," the Word said in a slightly husky voice.

The man's eyes cleared as he snapped out of his reverie. "Good morning!" he exclaimed. "How are you?"

"Better," the Word replied. "I feel weak, but better."

The Word was lying on a bed of straw. Light filtered into the room through a narrow window, and the shelves on the walls were piled high with tools. The Word saw little pick-axes, caesuras and hammers of all sizes, as well as iambic pentameters and wire brushes. There were also a pair of compasses hanging on a nail, and a verse metre ruler propped against the wall below it. The fire had burned down to ashes.

"My wife has been tending to you all night."

"What happened?" asked the Word.

"You can't remember, eh?" said the old man, turning towards the doorway. "*Rhyme*!" he called out. "My sonnet!"

The door opened and the woman from the night before came in carrying a large tray. "I heard you whispering. Has our guest woken up at last?" She squeezed past her husband and put the tray on the bed beside the Word. "Buttered toast, syllable salve and verbal tea. Just what the doctor ordered. I've yet to meet a word I haven't managed to cure with these. How are you feeling today, my dear?"

"Much better. Thank you."

"It can't remember anything," her husband chimed in.

Rhyme poured the tea into a large cup and handed it to the Word. "Nothing at all, hm?" She set to work, rubbing the salve into its syllables.

"Nothing at all," the Word replied. It paused for a moment, then said, "I don't know my own name."

"Listen," the man said, "you were spoken out loud. By a human."

The Word gulped. "A human?"

"Yes. We heard the shouts yesterday. I don't know where the other words ended up. You were the only one we found."

His wife screwed the cap back onto the tube of syllable salve. "It must have been a human," she said. "We haven't heard shouts like that in a very long time."

The next morning the Word felt strong enough to get out of bed. Its body still ached in places, but it felt a lot better. The old woman and her husband were nowhere to be seen. The Word ventured out of the room, which seemed to double up as a bedchamber and tool shed. In the next room was the kitchen, where two folded-up camp beds stood propped against the wall. Had the old couple let him sleep in their own bedroom? The Word heard a soft knocking sound. Then snatches of song:

> *"We too are chipped away by time,*
> *The hours must pass, the clock must chime,*
> *I seize the moments, hold them fast,*
> *And yet I know: this too shall pass."*

Slowly, the Word opened the door and stepped outside. The knocking grew louder. The garden was full of sculptures, about the same size as the Word itself. It followed the sound of the knocking, weaving its way through the rows of statues. Each one was a pair of sculptures carved from a single block of stone. On a brass plate at the foot of one of the pedestals, it saw two wordlets engraved: *Heart & Soul*. The Word looked at the pair of statues and realised that they depicted exactly that – one statue was carved into the shape of a heart, and the other was a flame burning straight and still, like a candle. Another sculpture consisted of a paper-thin sheet of stone with delicate lettering on it, and a seal with a tapering handle that looked rather like a bishop on a chess board. The brass plate beneath them read: *Signed & Sealed*. Word-pairs, thought the Word, and walked on through the garden of stone-art.

The knocking sounded much closer now, and the Word heard Rhyme's voice:

> *"In the end the book is shut*
> *And we are left with nothing but*
> *Empty silence, blank and still*
> *No here, no now, no we, no will."*

She must be standing right behind the two large statues the Word was now looking at. The sculpture was of a young couple. The man was down on one knee, clearly asking his sweetheart to marry him. The Word read the engraving on the plaque:

Rhyme & Reason.

Rhyme was sitting on a bench close by. She looked up from the sheet of paper she was holding and watched her husband work. Reason was standing in front of two hefty blocks of stone, chipping away at one of them with a hammer and chisel. When Rhyme caught sight of the Word, she beckoned it to come and sit beside her. The statue Reason was working on was nearly finished – it was a table with three words sitting around it, one of them reading the newspaper. A family having breakfast, thought the Word, and was overcome by melancholy without knowing why. The other block of stone was untouched. Reason had now put down his chisel and was in the process of attaching the brass plaque to the pedestal. The Word read …

… nothing.

The plaque was blank.

Reason lowered his hammer. "Finished," he said, although that was clearly not the case. Then he stepped closer to his wife and gave her a kiss. "That was a very moving poem, my love. What's it called?"

Rhyme thought for a moment and said, "I don't know. I don't think it has a name yet. Perhaps I've simply forgotten it, just as our guest here has forgotten its name. Things don't always need to have a name in order to be meaningful."

"What is this place?" enquired the Word.

Reason lowered himself slowly onto the bench beside his wife. "In all the years we've lived here, you're not the first word we've found lying in our fields. We've heard the shouts many times. I've been spoken out loud myself, you know. I was just a young man at the time."

"Did you lose your memory too?" asked the Word.

"No. I was quite badly hurt, but my memory wasn't affected. For me, the misfortune of being spoken out loud was actually the beginning of a wonderful story."

Rhyme gently placed her hand on Reason's thigh and started to speak. "I was just a young woman living here with my parents when I found him. He was gravely injured, and my mother and I nursed him back to health. As he gradually recovered, he started to tell me about all his ideas – about art, word sculpture and logic. His eyes shone as he spoke."

"And I loved your wonderful poems, my sonnet," said Reason, laughing. It made him look ten years younger. "A few weeks later, the first sculpture was complete."

"That was how he proposed to me," said Rhyme, pointing to the statue of the kneeling man which the Word had just been looking at.

"That's a lovely story," said the Word. Then, after a pause, it added, "And the other statues?"

Reason replied: "Whenever we found a word in the fields, a new sculpture was born. Sometimes it took years for them to be finished."

"Why do the statues all show pairs of words?" the Word asked.

"*Signed & sealed, safe & sound, live & learn, heart & soul, now & then,*" said Rhyme. "Every word, at a certain point in its life, may meet a companion – someone who completes it, who enables it to become something it never would have thought possible before. *Signed & sealed* became a *promise*. *Live & learn* became *wisdom*. *Heart & soul* became *devotion*. Not every word in the world has the good fortune to find such a partner, of course – but our word pairs, at least, are among the lucky ones."

The Word looked at the statue in front of them, the one it interpreted as a family sitting around the breakfast table, and again it was overcome by that feeling of melancholy which it couldn't quite explain. The other stone was still unworked and the brass plate blank. "You made this sculpture for me, didn't you?" it said. "Why a family?"

Reason stood up and went back over to his sculpture. He ran a hand over the rough surface of the uncarved stone. "The statues emerge all by themselves. I simply release what has always lain hidden within the stone. As a craftsman, you just know when something feels right. That's true not just of word sculptures, but of poetry too."

The Word wasn't sure it understood. "Why is one of the stones not sculpted yet?" it asked.

Rhyme put her arm around the Word. "Because, my dear, the stone hasn't yet told Reason what's hidden inside it. The first stone symbolises the beginning of your story, which is where you are now. The second stone symbolises the end. But nobody knows yet *how* your story will end. It didn't feel right to work on the sculpture yet."

Her husband continued: "Every word embodies its own name. My name is Reason, and that is who I am. You've forgotten your name and you've forgotten what you are. Just as I have found the rhyme to my reason, so you must find the end to your story. It might be an end you would never have thought possible before. Find out which word family you belong to. Because without family and without meaning, you are nothing."

The Word stayed with the old couple for a few more days. Rhyme insisted on applying the syllable salve every day, even though the pain had long since abated. But the Word's memory did not return. In the evenings, they sat around the fire while Reason told stories of the words he had already made into statues, and Rhyme recited poems in a soft whisper. The Word mostly stayed silent. It gazed into the fire and thought about what Reason had said. *Because without family and without meaning, you are nothing.* The thought went round and round in its head, keeping it awake for a long time that night before it finally drifted off to sleep.

The next morning, the Word took its leave of the old couple. "I will come back to see the finished sculpture, I promise," it told them. But it didn't know if it would be able to keep its promise. Rhyme insisted on giving the Word a parcel of provisions for the road, containing a hunk of bread and cheese and a flask of verbal tea. The Word accepted the parcel gratefully and set off, as Rhyme and Reason waved farewell. Reason had been right; it had to find out what it had forgotten, what its meaning was ...

... But where should it begin the search?

The Word was not the only one who hardly slept that night. In a completely different part of the world of language, two creatures had caught the scent of their next victim. That victim was a word without any meaning.

CHAPTER
THREE

A Mad Tea Party

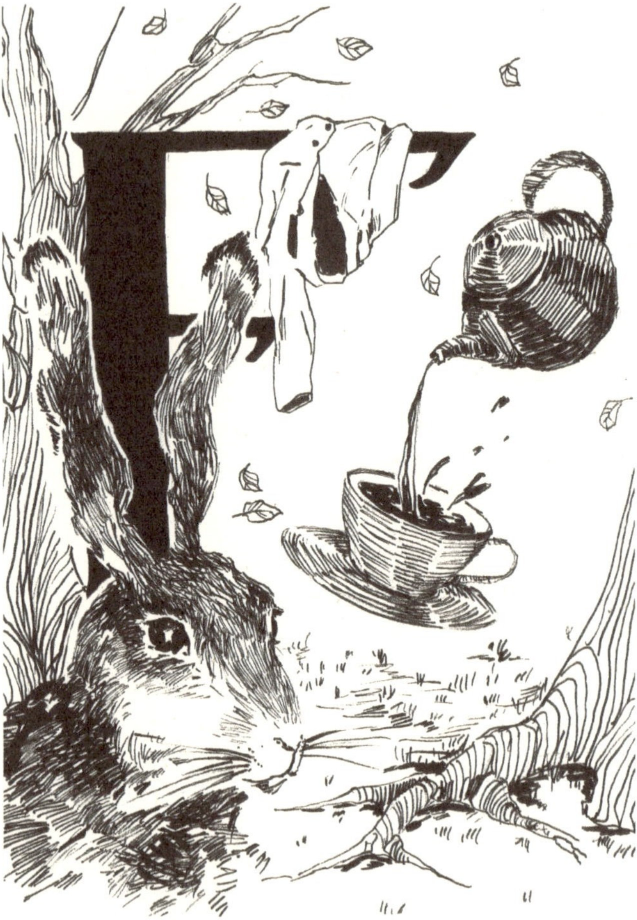
F

For two days now the Word hadn't seen another soul. It had finally reached the edge of a forest it had spotted on the horizon some time ago and had been travelling towards ever since. The Word sat down beside a stream to rest and quench its thirst. All it had left to eat now was a dry crust of bread, which it nibbled at slowly to make it last longer. Then it stood up and made its way into the forest.

It walked slowly into the shade of the beech trees whose reddish-orange leaves whispered and rustled like the yellowing pages of a book. With every step the Word took, twigs snapped underfoot. The forest smelt earthy, of fresh wood and ... tea? Was it imagining things? The Word pressed on through the undergrowth, pushing aside the brambles that blocked its path through the trees, following the scent. It stopped at the edge of a clearing and hid behind a tree trunk, where a strange sight met its eyes.

There was a round table in the middle of the clearing, laid with a white tablecloth and prepared for a tea party. Four little *h*'s were placed around the table. Upon two of these h's sat two large rabbits with grizzled, greying fur. They were sitting so still that you might have been forgiven for thinking they were asleep, except that their eyes were open and their noses twitched occasionally. White steam rose from a big silver teapot, beside which was a plate of biscuits.

The rabbits looked like amiable creatures, so the Word decided to go over and say hello. It stepped out from behind the tree and walked towards the rabbits. But just as the Word was about to open its mouth, it heard a loud yell. A word came bounding out of the trees and somersaulted across the clearing, coming to rest right in front of the Word. Then the stranger scrambled hastily to his feet and bowed. He was wearing a black suit, which he took off, as he bowed, to reveal a second suit – a white one this time. He tossed the old suit aside.

"Pleased to make your acquaintance. Would you like some black tea? You must be thirsty," the stranger asked politely, sitting down at the table.

"Oh, yes please! Black tea would be wonderful," said the Word, unfazed by the stranger's odd appearance.

"We only have herbal tea. A full pot of herbal tea," replied the stranger.

"Sorry, but why did you offer me black tea if you only have herbal tea?" asked the Word, confused.

"Everyone always wants black tea. No one ever asks for the herbal tea. So I call the herbal tea black tea. That way everyone gets what they want."

"You can't change something's name just because you feel

like it! If we don't know the proper names for things, it's just chaos!"

"Now, isn't that the pot calling the kettle black! You haven't yet told us *your* name yet." Then he poured out a steaming cup of herbal tea and handed it to the Word. The Word took a big sip of the tea, then popped a biscuit in its mouth.

"Shorry," said the Word with its mouth full.

"It's late," the stranger replied. "Let's get on with the game. We were just about to start playing. I'll go first, then you, then me again. All clear so far?"

"And what about the rabbits? When do they get a turn?"

"Rabbits?" the stranger exclaimed. "What rabbits?"

The Word pointed to the two rabbits sitting at the table. "Those rabbits," it said.

"Those aren't *rabbits*. Rabbits hide underground all day in their warrens. These two are very brave words, and incredibly fast runners: they used to reach speeds of up to 64 km/h when they were younger. They're *hares*. And Blackberry is not allowed to play."

"Why not?"

"Because all he ever does is talk about his watership. It's most irritating."

"A watership?" said the Word. "What's a watership?"

"Oh, don't you start!" cried the stranger, "or you won't be allowed to play either."

"Alright," said the Word, deciding not to dwell on it. "What about the other hare then?"

"If Blackberry isn't playing, Adam won't want to either. They're twins. Very elderly hares. Do everything together. The two of us will play by ourselves, taking it in turns."

The Word didn't understand. "But how can it be that you were just about to start playing if you didn't have anyone to play with?"

The stranger picked up the teapot, poured himself a cup of tea, took a loud slurping sip from it and looked straight at the Word. One of his eyes was open slightly wider than the other.

"A clever clogs, eh? But how do you know I didn't *know* you were coming to play with us? You're here, aren't you? And you're going to play with us? I'LL GO FIRST!" he shouted, and the Word felt rather alarmed. Its opponent really did seem very unpredictable.

The stranger grabbed the teapot again and spun it around in a circle. He sprayed tea all over his white suit in the process, but didn't even seem to notice. He looked at the teapot, lost in thought. Then he suddenly flung it up in the air and cried: "I've got it!"

The teapot landed with a crash among the exquisite china teacups, smashing them to smithereens. The hares were unperturbed. They just sat there twitching their noses. The Word was sorry to see the lovely teacups get broken, but didn't dare say anything. The stranger said euphorically: "I am white and black and very flat. What am I?"

Aha, thought the Word. A riddle. It knew this game. One player thought up a wordlet – it had to be a wordlet with multiple meanings – and gave the other players clues to help them guess what it was. Hopefully the stranger wasn't going to fly into a rage, because so far the Word had absolutely no idea what the answer was. What was white and black and very flat?

Then came the next clue, relating to the second meaning

of the wordlet. "I serve my master faithfully. What am I?" said the stranger.

The Word thought hard. Something that served its master faithfully – a sheepdog perhaps? Sheepdogs could be black and white. But they didn't tend to be very flat ... The Word needed another clue.

"We live on me. What am I?"

The Word had no idea. What did it live on that was black and white? "I give up. I don't know the answer, I'm sorry."

The stranger leapt to his feet again. He somersaulted onto his h and pulled off his tea-stained suit. Underneath it he was wearing a third suit, a black one again this time. He bellowed into the Word's face: "Great Scott, how can you still not know the answer?!"

The Word tried to stay calm. "I just don't. You tell me. What is it?"

"It's a page! A page serves his master faithfully. Pages in a book are often black and white, and we, the words, live on them."

The Word felt a headache coming on. "But we don't live on a page."

The stranger knocked over the little h he'd been sitting on, and roly-polied all the way around the table. When he stood up again, his suit was covered in green grass stains. Then he sat back down and said, "Of course we do. It's the humans, the humans who write us, who invent us. It's the humans. They write us on white sheets of paper, on pages, on the leaves of books. They write us, and we come to life! We live on their pages, in their imagination. It's the humans! They write us. On pages, on the leaves of books   " The stranger trailed off, grimacing as he spoke, and knocked over his h again. He hopped around the table on one leg while removing his suit to reveal yet another white suit. Then he returned the h to an upright position, sat down on it and seemed to regain his composure – for the moment, at least. "Your turn," he said quietly.

What on earth was this strange word talking about? The Word knew that humans spoke words aloud. It had painful first-hand experience of that. But to say that humans wrote words down was just nonsense! The stranger must be mad. It was probably best to play along, though. The Word was wary of its companion's reaction if it refused to join in the game. It thought for a while, trying to come up with its own riddle. And just then, carried towards them on the wind, came the soft sound of rushing water. It gave the Word an idea. "You can swim with me or against me. What am I?"

Like a juggler, the stranger held his hand palms upwards and moved them up and down as if to catch every wordlet that fell from the Word's lips. The Word continued: "I wasn't the past, I won't be the future, but I am the present. What am I?"

The stranger sprang up and shouted, "Present! You are the present! I've won!" He was delighted by his apparent victory. But of course the Word hadn't actually been thinking of the wordlet *present*. You cannot swim with or against the present. The answer to the riddle was in fact *current*. The Word didn't mention this to the stranger, however. Let him go on believing he'd won – at least then he'd be happy and leave the Word in peace. The stranger jumped up and down for joy, then bounded over to the hares and tugged on their ears. This brought them out of their trance, and they gazed at the stranger as he yelled, "I've won, I've won. Hear that,

Blackberry? Hear that, Adam?" He grabbed both the hares by their grey fur and shook them hard. "I've won!"

Then he sat down again and fell silent. The hares leant back on their h's and gave their friend a long look. Then they looked at the Word, who was timidly helping itself to another biscuit.

"Is it our turn then?" asked the hares simultaneously.

"Yes, it's your turn," replied the stranger cheerfully. "Tell us your riddle."

Encouraged by the stranger's sudden friendliness, the Word asked, "Didn't you just say Blackberry is not allowed to play because all he ever does is talk about his watership?"

The stranger leapt to his feet. "Great Scott, *must* you keep interrupting? It's Blackberry's turn now."

I should have just kept quiet, thought the Word, taking another biscuit.

"Our riddle is …" said Blackberry.

"… very interesting," Adam went on.

"*Very* interesting indeed," Blackberry repeated. "You'll need to listen carefully to the clues …"

"… in order to draw the correct inferences …" continued Adam.

"… and accurately deduce the answer to the riddle."

"Are you ready?" asked Blackberry.

The Word was impressed by the hares' eloquence. They seemed to finish one another's sentences without a second thought.

"We're ready," the Word and the stranger replied meekly.

Blackberry spoke in a voice as clear as a bell: "I'm said to drive hares mad, but in fact I do nothing of the sort. What am I?"

Now it was Adam's turn: "I am a route, trodden by many feet. What am I?"

The hares spoke way too quickly – the Word could hardly follow.

"I am the third of many ..." said Blackberry.

The stranger jumped up again and ripped off his suit with one quick movement. "I've got it!" he exclaimed.

The Word looked at him in surprise. The hares didn't seem particularly impressed.

"Well, what is it?" asked Adam.

The stranger clambered onto the table, stood on the white tablecloth amidst the wreckage of the broken tea service, and pointed triumphantly at the hares. "March! Ha!"

The hares were still unmoved. "You're right. Can you give an explanation?"

The stranger jumped down from the table and threw himself on the ground, then moved to sit back down on his h. "No, I can't. No, I won't! No! No! It's March. I know it is. No proof, no!"

As if he'd been expecting this, Blackberry said, "Very well. We will provide the proof then. We will prove your hypothesis by confirming ..."

"... the logical foundations upon which our riddle is based," Adam chimed in.

The hares have a very complicated way of expressing themselves, thought the Word, but it listened carefully to what they were saying. Why was March the answer to the riddle? It helped itself to another biscuit.

"The month of March is said to drive hares mad. Hence the saying: *as mad as a March hare*," Blackberry explained. "However, the month of March does not drive hares mad at all: the saying is based on the incorrect belief that at the beginning of the breeding season, male hares fight madly for breeding supremacy. In fact, the behaviour is quite reasonable: early in the season, unreceptive females often use their forelegs to repel overenthusiastic males. That is why it would make more sense to say: *as reasonable as a March doe*."

"Now we come to the second meaning," said Adam. "It's very simple. A march is a route trodden by many feet."

"And finally, ladies and gentlemen," Blackberry continued, "the month of March is the third of many – twelve to be precise. So there you have it: conclusive proof that your initial hypothesis was indeed correct. I offer you my warm congratulations, and hereby conclude my speech."

The stranger leapt up onto his little h and turned around, applauding admiringly in all directions. "What an outstanding speech. Quite outstanding. I couldn't have done it better myself. Clear, concise, informative. From the first second to the third – er – I mean, the first second to the last. Eye contact throughout. Not a hint of hesitation nor a soupcon of a stutter nor a whisker of a wobble. A triumph, I say. Bravo! Bravo!"

The hares were silent again, having seemingly fallen asleep with their eyes open. Their noses still twitched automatically. The stranger sat down again, and went so far as to offer the Word a biscuit. The Word politely declined – it had already eaten most of the biscuits on the plate and was quite full. Then the stranger rose from his chair and cleared his throat. "And now we come to a more solemn point in the proceedings." He pulled off his white suit to reveal another black suit. "We are gathered here today in order to discuss a serious matter."

The Word didn't know what the stranger was talking about, but it listened closely. It was gradually becoming fond of his madcap ways.

"We are gathered here today to talk about the problem."

"What problem?" asked the Word.

"Your problem," the stranger replied. "The hares and I have been watching you for quite some time now."

"You've been watching me?"

"Only for your own protection. Don't get the wrong idea about us. We're perfectly harmless, really. We're just interested in what goes on around the forest. And there was something about you that stood out."

"Tell me, then – what's going on? What is it that stands out about me?"

The stranger looked the Word in the eye and said, "Very well. But you might want to take a seat. I'm afraid you might start overreacting."

"I'm already sitting down," the Word replied drily.

"You, my dear, are being followed." And then the stranger leapt onto the table and shouted: "Followed! You're being followed! Fooolloooowed! FOLLOWED! Beware!"

"Followed? By whom?"

"Guess."

"Why do I have to guess? Is it a riddle?"

"Whatever gave you that idea? No, you're not being followed by a *riddle*. Now guess. It's a riddle."

"You'll have to give me a clue, then," the Word retorted.

The stranger snatched up the teapot again, gazed at it in fascination and then said, "I surround! I enclose! I separate! I destroy! What am I?" He sprang to his feet, threw his arms into the air and cried, "They're following us! They're following you! They've been following me! They're coming!"

The stranger started dashing back and forth between the trees, beating on their trunks with his fists, before running back to stand in front of the Word. He stammered: "They're f-f-f-following you. They're very c-c-close."

The Word had had enough now. "Pull yourself together! Who's following me?"

The stranger leaned in close to the Word's face, looked it in the eyes and stuttered, "Brack-br-brack... Br-brack..."

The Word grabbed hold of him and shook him. "Who? Tell me, now!"

The stranger's eyes were wild as he cried out, "The brackets!" Then he sat down again and fell silent.

"Brackets? What do you mean?" the Word asked incredulously.

"Ah, I thought you'd never ask!" the stranger exclaimed. "Allow me to introduce myself. I'm from a bohemian family: my father's name is *Nomad*, and my mother was a *Mademoiselle*. They had a passionate but ill-advised love affair, and I was the result." He put out his hand to the Word, who shook it. "Pleased to make your acquaintance. My name is *Mad*."

Things were finally starting to make sense.

"Pleased to meet you too, Mad. But what I actually wanted to know was, what did you mean by 'the brackets'?"

Mad tried to leap to his feet once more, but the Word had the presence of mind to grab his arm and hold him still.

"Bra-br-brack-brackets," Mad stammered. He sat down again, and the Word let go of his arm. "Brackets hunt down words that are no longer of any use to our world, or make it unnecessarily complicated. Filler words, which lengthen everything unnecessarily and which the brackets want to consign to the dustbin of history. But they won't catch me! They tried to erase me, but they won't catch me. I wasn't born yesterday. I've eliminated them. They want to get rid of me, all because I'm Mad. But they won't catch me." Mad was starting to repeat himself.

"What happens if the brackets find you?" asked the Word.

"They make you vanish without a trace. Just look at *betimes*, for example. Or *forsooth*. Two blameless little words I used to run into all the time. Then the brackets caught up with them. Since then, they've all but disappeared."

"But why were the brackets following you?"

"They didn't like my meaning. A mad word makes their world complicated. They're afraid humans won't understand me. The hares saved me. They're always so reasonable – and if you ask me …" Mad lowered his voice, "… they're a little bit boring, too. That's why it was important to have someone else in the forest, to even up the balance. Here, I make sense."

"And what makes you think *I'm* being followed?"

Mad replied, "For one thing, you look just like a word who's being followed by brackets. Pure coincidence brings you to our forest. You don't know what you're doing here or where you want to go. You haven't even told us who you are. I assume you've lost your meaning? Brackets love words like you. And for another thing, there's something in the bushes over there watching us," he added, as his darting eyes came to rest on a section of the undergrowth at the edge of the clearing. Mad bounded into the air, flailing madly, and in doing so knocked over not only his own h but all the h's around the table, sending himself, the Word and the hares tumbling to the ground.

"Brackets, brackets! The brackets are attacking!" he cried.

The hares slowly got to their feet, picked up their h's and sat back down on them. Mad went onto all fours and crawled over towards the bushes, from which the Word now saw two beady eyes peering out. A moment later, Mad leapt to his feet and bellowed at the top of his voice: "Come out and show yourself! I want to see the enemy!"

The bushes trembled. It sounded almost as though they were whimpering. And then a little creature scurried out and raised its tiny hands in surrender, as if begging for forgiveness.

"You're not a bracket," Mad remarked matter-of-factly, before returning to the table and seating himself calmly on one of the little h's.

The Word, still lying on the ground, stared at the little word that had come scuttling out of the bushes. It seemed familiar …

CHAPTER
FOUR

Watership Down

D

Daunted, the little word stepped out of the undergrowth with its hands still in the air. But when it saw the Word, a flash of recognition shone in its eyes. It trotted over to the Word, latched onto its left syllable, and clung on for dear life.

The Word had no idea what was happening. It looked down at the tiny creature, who gazed back expectantly.

"Mad! Hares! Could you come over here, please? What's going on?" the Word exclaimed in alarm.

Mad rose from his h, reached into his jacket pocket and took out a monocle which he placed over one eye, wedged between his eyebrow and his cheek. He came ambling over quite placidly. "What have we here then?" he murmured to himself. He examined the Word closely, walking around it so as to study it from every angle. "Interesting," he said, straightening his monocle. "Very interesting."

"Now tell me, Mad – what should I do?" pleaded the Word.

Mad put the monocle back in his pocket. "Blackberry, Adam, come over here a minute, since you both love explanations so much," he called.

The hares twitched their noses simultaneously and came hopping over.

"Pronouns, like this one," Mad pointed to the little word which was still firmly affixed to the Word's syllable, "are as common as leaves in the beech forest. But it's still extremely rare to actually catch a glimpse of one. They usually stay hidden. There are as many pronouns as there are nouns – and there are thousands and thousands of nouns. There are some right here in our clearing. Hares," Mad declared, addressing Blackberry and Adam, "you are nouns. Table," and here Mad turned and addressed the table, "you are a noun. And you,"

– he was speaking to the Word again – "you are a noun too."

The Word listened carefully as Mad went on: "Every noun in the world has a personal pronoun that belongs to it. At some point in their lives, the pronoun and the noun meet. This usually happens at a very young age, because the moment the pronoun is born, it sets off in search of its noun. A pronoun on its own doesn't mean much. It gets its meaning through symbiosis with its noun. Every word in the world of language has its own meaning, and these little fellows are keen to find their place in life too, as soon as they can. And in turn, nouns are made complete through symbiosis with their pronoun. They come of age."

"Are you a noun, too?" asked the Word.

"No, I'm not," Mad replied.

"What are you, then?"

"I'm Mad. That's all I am, and I'm perfectly happy that way, thank you very much. The main thing is that your pronoun has found you."

The Word didn't understand. "What makes you think it's *my* pronoun?"

"It must be yours. Why else do you think it's clinging to your syllable like that?"

Now Blackberry broke in. "You've explained it all very well, Mad. But now ..."

"... let's get on with the symbiosis," said Adam.

Mad grinned. He started running in circles around the table, beating his chest and crying, "Swear the oath! Swear the oath! Swear the oath!" By this time, Mad had no idea whether he was wearing a white suit or a black one. He ripped off his jacket and trousers to reveal his last and best suit, a smart white one. He was about to initiate the symbiosis. The hares each picked up an h off the ground and sat down. The wind rustled through the beech trees and the sunlight came filtering through the leaves. Mad spoke solemnly: "Pronoun, Word, stand and face each other. Look each other in the eye."

The pronoun let go of the Word and took a few steps backwards.

"We are gathered here today to join together two words," Mad announced. "Pronouns are so small that they cannot be broken up. And in the same way, the oath which these two words are about to swear shall remain unbroken."

It was very quiet in the clearing now. Even the hares' noses had stopped twitching as they held their breaths in anticipation. Then Mad spoke. "Word, do you swear to honour your pronoun, for better or for worse? Repeat after me: Yes, I will honour my word."

The Word hesitated for a moment. It looked at the pronoun standing before it, which still felt so familiar, and said, "Yes, I will honour my word."

"And you, pronoun, do you swear to honour this Word, for better or for worse? If you do, tell us your name, or forever hold your peace."

"She," the pronoun replied in a squeaky little voice.

Mad seemed pleased with himself. He looked solemnly at each of them in turn, before proclaiming, "Then, by the power I have vested in myself, I now pronounce you pronoun and noun. You may now honour your word."

The pronoun took a few steps forward and embraced the Word, who had knelt down to be closer to it. The pronoun melted into the embrace, fused with its noun and became part of it. The pronoun had disappeared.

"What happened?" asked the Word. "Where is it?"

Blackberry clapped his front paws together. "The symbiosis was successful," he said. "Congratulations! You are now united with your personal pronoun. You are a noun. A feminine one."

The Word didn't realise she'd been joined with her pronoun once before, back when she was still living with her parents. The human who'd spoken her had separated her from her pronoun, and she'd lost her memory after the fall. And yet the little pronoun had still seemed strangely familiar to her. The Word was one step closer to finding her meaning. She now knew that she was a feminine noun. So much had happened since the accident. How had she ended up on this bizarre adventure? Rhyme and Reason, Mad and the hares – what did any of that have to do with her?

"Hares, Mad," she said determinedly, "tell me what I should do. Where should I go?"

Mad was about to reply, but the hares interrupted him.

"You must go away ..."

"... Away from here."

"But where to? I have to find out what I've forgotten, and what my meaning is. I just don't know where to look for it."

"There are thousands of paths for you to take. Recognising the path that gives you meaning is the greatest challenge of all."

"But where should I start?"

The two hares got slowly to their feet and went lolloping off towards the edge of the clearing. Blackberry looked back over his shoulder as he went, and called: "Come on. We want to show you something."

The Word followed them, with Mad shuffling along behind. They made their way through a part of the beech forest the Word had not seen before. At first, they made slow progress through the thick undergrowth, but after a while the bushes and brambles started to thin out. The sound of rushing water filled the air. At last they emerged from the trees and stopped on the bank of a wide, fast-flowing river. The Word could hardly believe her eyes.

"My goodness," she whispered, awestruck.

The hares turned around as one, and gazed serenely at the Word. Mad had seen the sight that lay before them many times before, but it still took his breath away.

"The hares' watership," he breathed.

An iron chain stretched across the river. On the bank, mounted on a sturdy wooden structure, was a pulley system to which the chain was attached. Floating on the water was a raft made from several tree trunks held together with thick ropes. The raft was attached to the iron chain by guide rails leading across the river. The water flowed quickly, churning into white foam around the tree trunks, but the raft didn't move. It floated beside the bank as if rooted to the spot.

"There it is," said Blackberry.

"Our watership," said Adam.

"It's amazing," murmured the Word.

Then the hares spoke as if with one voice, each finishing the other's sentences.

"You asked where you should go to find your meaning. One thing's for certain: you can't stay here. Leave the beech forest. Cross the river. We don't know what awaits you on the other side. We've never been beyond the riverbank. No desire to. No need to. Our adventuring days are over. Now we're just a pair of old hares who've finally found their home. We like sitting in our clearing, drinking tea. Eating biscuits. Guessing riddles. And when we don't feel like doing that, we just sit there twitching our noses. Every so often, a word comes along wanting to cross the river in our watership and that's fine. That's enough meaning for us. We don't need any more than that. But you must leave this place. You won't find your meaning here. With every step you take, you make a decision, for in taking that step you rule out countless other possibilities you might also have chosen. The secret is to decide. And with every decision you make in life, you take a step forward."

Mad looked sideways at the hares, his eyes wide.

They were right, the Word knew it. She had to move on, otherwise she would never find out what her meaning was. It didn't really matter where she went: whichever path she took, she would be further along than she was now.

"Thank you for letting me use your watership," she said to the hares.

The hares nodded in unison. Then the Word turned to Mad. "Mad, it was a great pleasure to meet you." She smiled and added, "There's never a dull moment with you around."

"You'll find your meaning eventually," Mad replied, "I'm sure of it. Everyone makes sense, even a nonsense like me. Otherwise, you know, I'd never have been written down. Believe it or not, you too were written down once. Or perhaps you're being written down right now. So you must have a meaning. Sense or nonsense, meaningful or meaningless – who gets to decide these things? Personally, I like changing my suits eleven times a day, doing somersaults and making sure the hares don't get too bored. That's what defines me. As long as I'm surprising, entertaining and puzzling, as long as I have imagination, I also have meaning. That's how I see it, anyway. Remember that. Without imagination, most things are pretty boring. Everyday life, the same old routine day in day out. For me, ordinariness is the biggest nonsense of all."

Mad gave the Word a hug. She didn't know what to make of this strange fellow. He said such funny things. But perhaps she ought to take him more seriously, despite his odd ways. Perhaps he wasn't a madman, but a dreamer. The Word thanked Mad and the hares once more and turned away to step slowly onto the raft. Blackberry and Adam went over to the pulley and started turning the crank to wind in the chain. With every turn, the watership advanced a little way across the river.

When the Word had reached the middle of the river, Blackberry drew out a shard of broken china from the tea set. With two deep cuts, he sawed the pulley rope in two. With a loud clatter the iron chain unravelled, leaving the raft at the mercy of the current. The Word tried to cling onto the base of the watership, but there was nothing to hold onto. The raft rocked wildly as it floated ever further downstream.

Water washed over the tree trunks, making them so slippery that the Word lost her grip and slid off into the river. Soon she would be engulfed by the powerful torrents. Her cries for help were almost drowned out by the churning water.

The hares watched impassively as the Word was swept away. "Good luck," they chorused softly.

The two creatures who'd been following the Word were still on her scent. They raced across a field, paused for a moment to be sure, then hastened on towards a forest in the middle of which lay a clearing. The table standing in the clearing was not laid. Four h's were arranged neatly around the table. The clearing was deserted, but the scent of one of their future victims still hung in the air. It was a meaningless scent, one that could only have come from a word which was completely meaningless or had lost its meaning a long time ago. The two creatures wasted no time. They followed the scent, which led them through the forest to a wide, fast-flowing river. At the water's edge floated a raft, fixed to an iron chain that stretched across to the opposite bank. Here the trail went cold. They took each other's hands for a moment, seemed to come to a decision, and stepped onto the raft. After a few strong tugs on the chain they had reached the other side.

CHAPTER
FIVE

In the Torrent of Words

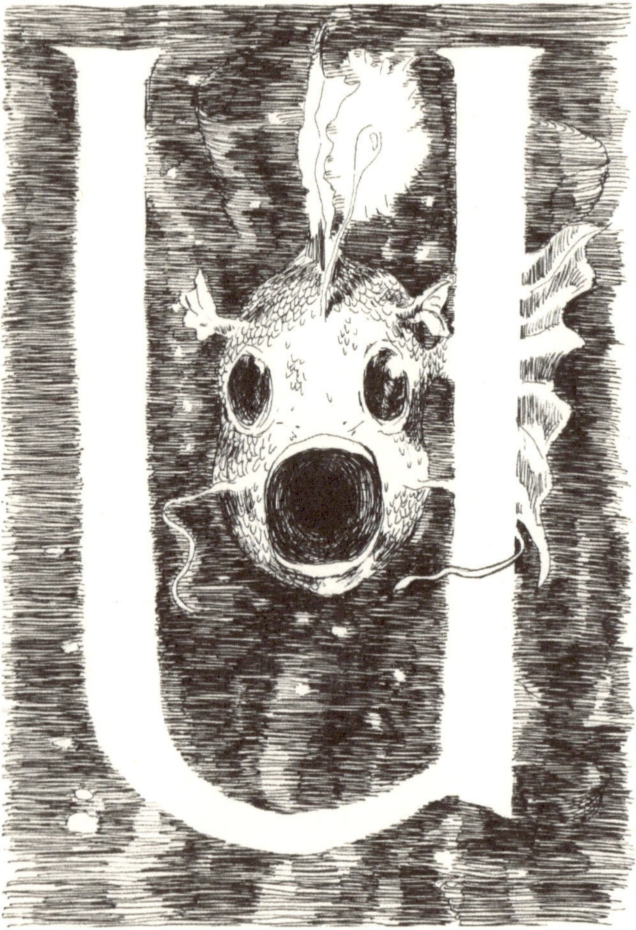

Under the water, the Word found herself surrounded by a current of words who tugged at her syllables as they flowed past her. They got caught up in each other, composed loose sentences that broke up as quickly as they'd formed. The force of the current dragged her down, only to wash her back up to the choppy surface a moment later as it carried her swiftly downstream. The Word tried to grab onto the vegetation growing on the bank, but her grip kept slipping. A little way ahead of her, the river was frothing and churning. A narcissistic whirlpool was making all the words revolve around it. The Word was headed straight for the whirlpool – any moment now, it would swallow her up. The Word stayed on the surface for an instant, no more than white noise, before the whirlpool dragged her down into the depths with the other words. The light from the surface faded into the distance. She could only vaguely make out the words around her. A hand brushed hers, and she clasped it instinctively. Together with the unknown word whose hand she was holding, she sank down into the depths below.

"Can you hear me?" she said into the surrounding silence.

"Yes, but I can't see a thing," replied the word beside her.

"What's your name?"

"*Looking-Glass*. And yours?"

"I've forgotten my name."

"I'm sorry."

The Word didn't want to dwell on the subject. Instead, she said, "Looking-Glass is an unusual name."

"It's a very old name. The word *mirror* is more common these days. Hardly anyone remembers the *looking-glass*."

The current pulled them deeper and deeper. The light barely penetrated down here at all.

"I've never been this deep before," said Looking-Glass. "This is the realm of dead language."

"Dead language?" the Word echoed.

"This is where the archaisms live. Methuselah words."

The current was slowing down. At last, the Word felt solid ground beneath her feet. The water around them was pitch black.

"What are Methuselah words?" she asked, still holding Looking-Glass's hand very tightly.

"They're the oldest words in our world. Thousands of years old."

"We shouldn't stay here. I've got a bad feeling about this," said the Word.

At that moment, a halo of light appeared in the darkness, then another, and another. At first the Word was quite dazzled by them, but then the world around her began to take shape. Where the light illuminated the depths, she could see a shoal of giant turtles floating in the water, drifting almost imperceptibly – barely moving. The heads and limbs that protruded from their dark shells were motionless too. The light came from the anglerfish that had settled on top of the turtles' shells. One of the fish was very close to the Word, for she and Looking-Glass had also landed on the back of one of the turtles. The shell beneath them trembled, and from inside it came a rumbling voice.

"Grandpapa's lanterns, blazing since time immemorial. As effulgent as they ever were. *The Wise Old Wherefore* is confounded by it."

"What did she say?" asked the Word, who had only understood a fraction of the wordlets issuing from the shell.

Looking-Glass hesitated for a brief moment. "They're her

grandad's lamps," he translated. "The Wise Old Wherefore is amazed that they still shine so brightly."

"The Wise Old Wherefore?"

"That's what she calls herself."

"How can you understand what she says?"

"I don't understand all of it. But I remember some of her wordlets from when I was young. We used to say Grandpapa instead of Grandad too. Methuselah words sometimes use dead language. They forget that lots of wordlets died out a long time ago."

There came a rumble of protest from beneath them.

"Heaven forfend! The Wise Old Wherefore does not forget! Nary a word! Zounds, the presumptuousness of youth, seeking to pierce the silence of these pitchy depths. Oh, forebear from such villainy!"

"What?"

Looking-Glass whispered, "She's saying we should be silent down here in the dark depths of the river. I shouldn't have said anything about wordlets dying out. That offended her."

"Why do we have to be silent?" asked the Word.

From underneath them came a creaking, grating sound. Very slowly, a scaly head emerged from the shell and twisted its long neck to stare directly at the two words sitting on its back. Its tiny nose, which was dwarfed by the rest of its face, was all of a piece with its forehead. Its black eyes were set wide apart. Its mouth was a thin line surrounded by a mass of wrinkles. The passage of time was etched deeply into this face.

"Only in tenebrous quietude can Wherefore bethink herself aright!"

"She can only think properly in darkness and silence," Looking-Glass interpreted in a whisper.

The turtle moved her head until it was very close to Looking-Glass. Then she said, "The Wise Old Wherefore has no need of this young pipsqueak of a word, who is not yet full grown, to translate what she says. Wherefore knows *all* wordlets. Wherefore does not forget."

The Word turned to the turtle. "I'm sorry that we've disturbed you. What were you thinking about?"

The turtle's gaze rested on her. "Today, Wherefore has bethought herself of Death. Such a little word, is it not? And yet so hardy. As old as the hills. But still it floats upon the surface of the torrent. The years have barely altered it. Wherefore wonders when Death will sink down to join her."

The Word understood what the turtle was saying this time, but she still didn't know what to make of it. "I don't understand. When do words sink to the bottom of the river?"

"When they grow old and are forgotten," the turtle replied. "The *mirror* replaces the *looking-glass*. The *thief* replaces the *cutpurse*. The *cat* replaces the *grimalkin*. When nobody remembers them any longer, they sink beneath the surface of the torrent and end up here."

"And how do they get back to the surface?"

"Back? They do not get back! Once they enter the realm of dead language, they stay here at the bottom of the river forever."

The Word glanced at Looking-Glass. "But there must be some way of stopping it from happening?"

"Hmm, mayhap, mayhap. But Wherefore must ponder that awhile," the turtle replied. Then she closed her eyes and fell silent. The Word looked doubtfully at Looking-Glass.

Several minutes went by without the turtle saying anything.

"Wherefore!" called the Word. And since the turtle didn't respond, she called again: "Wherefore!"

Slowly, the Wise Old Wherefore opened her eyes. "Do you still seek to pierce the silence?!" she said.

"How do we get back to the surface?"

"Wherefore has already told you, she needs to ponder that awhile. It behoves you both to do likewise, and engage in quiet contemplation."

"What should we contemplate?" asked the Word.

"Your own meaning, perhaps?" returned the Wise Old Wherefore. "A splendid subject. Very complex. It will keep you well occupied for years to come."

"What do you know about my meaning?"

"You are a young word, is that not so? Highly impatient. All young words seek meaning. Wherefore was young once too, and could not navigate the torrent fast enough. She wanted to reach the mouth of the river, to leave traces where nobody had been before. She thought she would live forever. And she failed to notice that she was gradually ageing. Eventually, *Wherefore* was replaced by *Why*. She sank beneath the surface and became an archaism: the Wise Old Wherefore. Why is still floating on the surface. But even he has aged by this time. He too will descend to the riverbed one day, to be replaced by a younger word."

"How do we get back to the surface?" the Word asked once more. But the Wise Old Wherefore was lost in thought again.

"It's not so terrible, now, is it? Wherefore has lived a rich and full life. She has known happiness. She has been loved, and has loved in return. The world of language is constantly in flux. Some words that float on the water's surface today will be forgotten in a hundred years. For years, Wherefore thought she would arrive somewhere sooner or later. But she was wrong. The river has no mouth. The torrent flows on and on forever, merely with different words at its surface."

"But how do we get back to the surface?"

"You are too young, it is true. You did not deserve to be forgotten. You descended into the depths along with Looking-Glass."

"I didn't mean to pull her under!" cried Looking-Glass.

"How do we get back?" asked the Word again.

Still deep in thought, the Wise Old Wherefore murmured, "Sometimes, by chance, we come across wordlets that are already half-forgotten, do we not? In an old book, or in a tale someone is telling us. The half-forgotten wordlet comes back to life for as long as the story lasts. And if the story makes an impression on us, we go off and retell it to somebody else. It is passed from word to word, from place to place. And as we tell the story, the half-forgotten wordlet comes back into our minds. As time goes on, it is no longer forgotten. It comes alive again. Perhaps that is not only true of wordlets – perhaps it might be true of Looking-Glass too? If he were to appear in a story, then Looking-Glass would also be able to rise to the surface of the torrent again, would he not?"

The turtle was silent for a moment, seemingly reflecting on what she'd just said. Then she started chanting in a monotonous voice, "Looking-Glass. Looking-Glass. Looking-Glass. Looking-Glass. Looking-Glass …"

At first, nothing happened.

"Looking-Glass. Looking-Glass …"

Suddenly, the Word felt a gentle force tugging at her.

"What are you doing?" cried Looking-Glass, but at that very moment all three of his syllables came away from the turtle's shell. Looking-Glass began to float slowly upwards.

"Take my hand," he called to the Word, who wasted no time in grabbing the hand Looking-Glass had extended to her. The current had caught both of the words now, and was propelling them steadily towards the surface.

"What's happening?" the Word cried, looking down at the turtle.

The Wise Old Wherefore gazed up at the words, who were already quite some way away. Lost in thought, she answered: "You seem to be part of a story. But Wherefore must ponder that awhile." And with that, the Wise Old Wherefore withdrew into her shell. The anglerfishes' lights went out, and the depths were plunged into darkness once more.

The Word wasn't sure she fully understood what the old turtle had said. But she called back, "Farewell!" as she and Looking-Glass drifted further and further away.

Holding hands, the two words floated higher and higher to where even stronger currents began to pull at them. The Word saw the outlines of other words being swept along by the torrent. There was a shoal of monosyllabic fish, arranging themselves succinctly into terse sentences. Stressed syllables swam past, floundering about in the water and looking worried. Sing-song cadences sang songs about anglerfish fishing for compliments. And then a flurry of foreign words went by, pursued by a babel fish.

Did all these words know that their time was running out, and that eventually they would sink beneath the surface of the torrent of words?

They were only a few moments away from the surface now. The current buoyed them up and out of the water, and they fell into each other's arms.

"I thought we'd have to stay down there forever," said Looking-Glass. "What happened?"

"I suppose you must not be as old as you look," the Word replied, feeling very relieved herself.

As they were talking, they drifted further downstream, past little whirlpools that they just about managed to avoid being sucked into.

"I wonder how much time I've got left before I do finally sink to the bottom of the river," mused Looking-Glass.

"We'll all end up as turtles swimming around at the bottom of the river one day. Then we'll all be old and wise. You'll be Wise Old Looking-Glass, and I'll be Wise Old …"

"You still don't know what your name is, do you?" said Looking-Glass.

"No," the Word replied.

"Look!" cried Looking-Glass all of a sudden. The Word saw it too. In the distance loomed a dark stone wall, behind which grey towers jutted into the sky.

"A city," said Looking-Glass. "The torrent of words runs right past the city wall. You have to leave the water here."

"How?" asked the Word.

"This is the perfect place. I've been past walls like this before. There are steps set into the stone, leading all the way down to the water. The words from the cities use them when they need to repair the wall. When we float past, you'll have to grab onto the handrail and pull yourself up before your strength fails you."

"What about you?"

"I'm staying here," said Looking-Glass.

"Come with me. Otherwise, sooner or later, you're going to sink to the bottom again."

"Like you said, sooner or later we're all going to sink to the bottom. So I'm staying here. The torrent doesn't distinguish between words, however meaningful or meaningless they may seem. Here, we're all of equal significance."

The torrent had carried them so close to the wall that they could see the steps, spaced wide apart, leading up to the top.

"Are you ready?" asked Looking-Glass, clasping the Word's hand.

"Yes." And then they found themselves pressed up against the wall. The Word could feel the smooth stone. Other words came tumbling up behind them, pushing them along the wall. The handrail of the first set of steps went rushing past. The Word hadn't even tried to grab hold of it. Looking-Glass pointed to the next flight of steps, which was still some way ahead of them.

"You didn't go under in the torrent of words, so don't let them get you down up there either, okay?" Then Looking-Glass thrust the Word towards the wall, against the direction of the current, and at the same time let go of her hand. For a moment the Word was dragged underwater, and everything slowed down. But then she bobbed up right in front of the steps and grabbed onto the metal handrail. She felt the tug of the current fall away. With her last ounce of strength, she hauled herself up onto the first step. Looking-Glass had disappeared – the torrent of words raced on. The Word slowly climbed the steps. When she reached the top, she had a view of the entire city. The sight took her breath away.

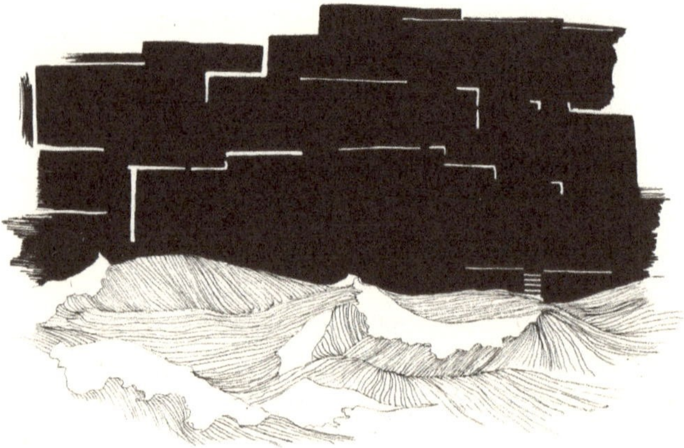

CHAPTER
SIX

Langwich

WELCOME TO LANGWICH, THE HOME OF THE LINGUISTIC GAMES

From her vantage point on top of the wall, the Word gazed out over the city, which was spread out like a vast grey carpet across the land. But it wasn't like one of those finely woven oriental carpets – more like a dusty doormat thrown carelessly outside the door into the cold night. A maze of roads, which had sprung up separately long ago but which now criss-crossed all over the city, separated the different districts. On the horizon, a haze of fine dust rose from the high chimneys and shimmered in the sun. The streets were full of words travelling towards the centre of the city. From where she was standing, the Word couldn't quite make out what was at the city's centre. It looked like a white hole that was gradually absorbing all the words. A flight of steps led down the wall and into the city.

The Word was rudely jolted out of her reverie by someone shoving her to one side in their hurry to descend the steps.

"Look out, will you!" cried an ox with curly horns. "Don't just stand there – you're holding up the traffic!" Other words pushed and jostled behind the ox.

"Come on! What's taking so long?" called out a word from somewhere further back in the crowd.

"Calm down! We all want to get where we're going!" retorted a cactus, whom the other words were giving a very wide berth.

A crane with a squeaking wooden pulley, standing near the front, craned its neck for a better view and called back, "We're coming up to a language junction – there are some translation works going on!"

The Word had reached the bottom of the steps by this time, and got caught up in the throng of words surging slowly towards the city centre. Their route took them through narrow lanes, past little shops selling all kinds of curious items in all kinds of curious ways. She spotted a stall piled high with goods, where the market crier – a bad-tempered imperative – was yelling at the top of his voice, "Wash, cloths! Paint, brushes! Cook, books!" But the cloths, brushes and books didn't respond, and the words in the crowd all did their best to steer clear of the merchant too.

On a street corner, an artist was painting a reclining figure of speech. The artist's smock was covered in dabs of dried oil paint. Beside his easel was a queue of other idioms waiting to have their portraits painted – a *tall tale* was next in line, followed by a *sacred cow*, a *pig in a poke* and a *one-trick pony*. The artist must have just completed his latest portrait, because he was taking the canvas off the easel and handing it to a rather ugly-looking idiom. The canvas was completely blank.

"What's this?" asked the idiom who'd just had its portrait painted.

"*No oil painting*," replied the artist.

"I shouldn't have told you my name!" laughed the idiom, handing the artist a shilling and walking off with the canvas.

The words advanced slowly until they reached another junction. Suspended above the junction was a friendly sentence. A meticulous workman was perched on a ladder, busy dotting the *i*'s and crossing the *t*'s. The t's were already finished, but the workman hadn't started on the i's yet. The sentence read:

Welcome to Langwich, the home of the Linguistic Games. ....

In addition to the full stop, the four dots for the i's were balanced at the end of the sentence ready for the workman to pick up. This was causing a bit of a problem for the sentence structure, which was wobbling violently.

A policeman in uniform was directing the traffic across the junction. With rapid movements, he turned and gestured to the words when to go and when to stop. He blew his whistle, but the sound was completely drowned out by the hubbub around him. Now he waved through the cluster of words in which the Word found herself. Once they were past the junction, the throng gained momentum. The cactus who had overtaken the Word only a few moments ago was already some way ahead of her. The Word wasn't in a hurry, and let herself be carried along by the crowd. She looked all around her and marvelled at the city of Langwich, with all its citizens and its buildings. By the side of the road, she spotted a figure wrapped in a shining golden cloak – a poem. A well-dressed pen tossed a few coins into the poem's cap, which he'd placed on the ground in front of him. Now some of the words stopped and gathered around the poem, who stood up and spread his arms wide, making his golden cloak look all the more impressive. He stared straight ahead, closed his eyes and declaimed:

"The Pen

He trembles across the sheet of paper,
Writes and writes for his life,
Lends form to imagination; captures it
And divides it into wordlets.

Every wordlet is shaped by him

...

Given wings by him,
Sent on journeys
From place to place.

Take me with you,
Write me down.
Surrounded by fairy tales,
In this unlikely town."

Then he sat down again and was silent. There was a smattering of applause before the words quickly moved off again. They bustled about, weaving deftly around each other. Some stopped at the little stalls where jewellers sold silver tongues and golden silences, and confectioners peddled vox popcorn and sugar-coated truths. Others paused to have their shoes shone by a little bootblack waxing lyrical in a shop doorway. Several lingered to listen to an exclamation mark who was standing on a soapbox making an impassioned speech, and a few stopped to talk to a performance poet who was giving away free verse. But most pressed on towards the city centre, the Word among them. Soon they had reached their destination.

The centre of Langwich was situated on lower ground than the rest of the city, giving you a good view of it even before you reached it. In the middle of the central square was a dome, and all the way around its circumference were dark wooden doors set into its stone walls. The roof of the dome consisted of white flagstones – this was what the Word had taken for a big white hole when she'd seen it form high up on the wall. The square was full of words jostling each other towards the doors.

"What's going on?" the Word wondered aloud.

"Those are the ticket barriers for the Linguistic Games," whispered a voice from behind her.

The Word turned around, and was startled to see a bird with a large curved beak standing before her. He had a fat round body, bluish-grey feathers and short, stubby wings, with which he was leaning on a dainty wooden cane. His sulphur-yellow eyes on either side of his leathery head were opened a touch too wide. The two black pinpricks in the middle were trained on the Word.

"You're not from these parts," the bird observed.

"No, I'm not."

"Do you see the guards over there?" he asked.

She turned and looked towards the central square. "Yes, I see them."

Several watchwords were guarding the doors. From a distance it was hard to make out what they were, but she thought she saw a hippopotamus, and next to it an albatross.

"The watchwords are checking the tickets. You can't get in without a ticket. Have you a ticket?" His yellow eyes glinted.

"No, I haven't," the Word replied. The bird's beak opened slightly to reveal a swollen black tongue.

"Then today is your lucky day," he exclaimed. "Please allow me to introduce myself. My name is *Charles Lutwidge Dodgson*. My companion has, unfortunately, been detained. But I should be delighted if you would accompany me in her place." As he spoke, he drew two printed slips of paper out of his neck pouch.

Charles Lutwidge Dodgson – that was one of the strangest names she'd ever heard, thought the Word.

"I don't have any money," she said.

"Oh, no, no, no! I wouldn't hear of your giving me any money. The ticket is a gift. Come with me to the Linguistic Games. It'll be such fun."

"That's very kind of you, but I can't possibly accept."

"Oh but you can," he whispered in her ear, slipping his stumpy little wing through her syllable and steering her towards the doors. "Make sure that you stay close to me. There are rumours all over the city. Apparently several words have gone missing."

"Missing?"

"The Linguistic Games attract all kinds of meaningless words. Beggars and buskers, punsters and poetasters, peddlers of wisecracks and one-liners – wretched creatures all. The city is always full of them during the Linguistic Games. And a few of them are said to have gone missing."

The Word remembered the poem by the side of the road. Poems weren't meaningless, she thought.

They had to wait quite a long time to get to the front of the queue, where a huge oak tree loomed between them and the door. The bird handed over their tickets.

"The girl can go in." The oak's booming voice filtered down from somewhere high up in his majestic leafy crown.

"But you ..." The tree grabbed the bird with one of his branches and shook him. Failing to find anything suspicious, however, he set him down again and waved him through the door, which swung open with a low groan. It was pitch black inside. Only occasionally did a shaft of light pierce the darkness as one or other of the doors opened.

"Come along," whispered the bird, drawing the Word deeper into the darkness.

Then suddenly she couldn't feel the ground beneath her feet anymore. As they fell further and further downwards, she clung to the bird's feathers and heard indistinct scraps of other words falling alongside them. But although they fell for a very long time, they didn't crash-land – quite the opposite, in fact. One minute they were still plunging through the air, the next they fetched up on the ground, landing with a soft bump. They found themselves in a dimly candlelit tunnel. Words were visible in the gloom, but they all seemed eager to be on their way. Above the ground, the city's central square had been full of words, but this place was practically empty. Even though new words materialised from time to time, they soon vanished into the mouth of the tunnel.

"Come along, let's go," prodded the bird beside her.

"Where are we going?" she asked.

"To the Linguistic Games, of course," he answered, pulling her along with him.

The tunnel was long and winding, with side tunnels branching off from the main thoroughfare in places. The bird insisted on taking these short-cuts.

The Word lost her sense of direction and blindly followed her companion through the tunnels. They came across fewer and fewer words until, having taken countless turns, they found themselves in an utterly deserted tunnel. The bird stood still, turned to face her and gazed at her with his sulphur-yellow eyes.

"What is it?" she asked.

"I was just thinking ..." the bird began.

"What?"

"You're beautiful," he whispered, "so beautiful."

She recoiled.

"We're all alone, you know ..."

The Word took a step backwards and felt the cold wall of the tunnel behind her. The bird came closer.

"Her skin shimmers like silver. I long to kiss her mouth. Love. Oh, warmth. Such soft cheeks, round and smooth. Those tumbling locks. I shall catch them. In my arms. If I could only stroke her hair. Look at her hands, so natural. Love." His eyes gleamed.

"Leave me alone!" she cried, pushing him away.

But he went on in a fanatical whisper: "For her, I am a companion. Feelings not reciprocated. I long for her. Believe my lies."

"Help! HEEEELP!" she yelled, as loudly as she could.

"It would feel good. So good. For the two of us. A little togetherness. A moment. And you would be mine."

Just then, someone clubbed the bird over the head with a heavy branch and sent him toppling to the ground.

Holding the branch was a giant. The sorry creature fell with a muffled thud and lay unconscious at their feet. The giant must have been crouching very low as he'd crept towards them, but as he'd struck the bird he'd drawn himself up to his full height. He was at least three times as tall as the Word.

"I'd advise you to steer clear of scoundrels like this," said a voice, which didn't sound like that of a giant.

The giant stepped silently aside, and another word came into view. He was dressed in a robe the colour of yellowing paper, and the scales on his head were reddish-brown, like a copper suit of armour.

"Do you know who that is?" asked the lizard, pointing to the bird, who still lay inert on the ground.

"Ch... Charles Ludwich Dodgesun, or something like that," the Word stammered, fighting back tears.

"Hmm. Is that what he told you?"

"Ye... yes."

"Charles Lutwidge Dodgson was a great storyteller. He has nothing whatsoever in common with that bird."

The Word had no idea what he was talking about.

"The bird's name is *Lust*," said the lizard. "Please accept my apologies. The watchwords try to make sure words like this are denied access to the Games. But you saw how chaotic it was up there. Mistakes get made."

"I shouldn't have gone with him. I thought there was something strange about him," said the Word.

The lizard turned to the giant. "*Defiance*, get him out of here and make sure he never sets foot in Langwich again."

The giant nodded, slung the bird effortlessly over one shoulder and disappeared into the maze of tunnels.

"Do you work here?" asked the Word.

The lizard seemed slightly confused by this question. "Yes. Again, please accept my apologies. The Linguistic Games are supposed to be a happy occasion." He reached into his robe and soon found what he was looking for. In his hand was a golden ticket. "Here, take this. You'll have one of the best seats in the house."

The Word took the ticket and thanked the lizard. "I'm intrigued to see what the Linguistic Games are all about."

"You've never been to the Games before?"

"No."

"Well then, we'd better get going! Come on, I'll show you the way back."

The Word followed him through the tunnels. After a while they began to pass little clusters of words here and there. As they passed, the words nudged and whispered to each other. The Word and the lizard ignored them, and soon arrived back at the main tunnel.

"From here, just go straight on and you'll see the ushers. Show them your ticket, and enjoy the evening."

"Are you going to watch the Games too?"

"Yes – I've got a prime spot," the lizard replied with a smile. "Have fun!" Then he disappeared into one of the side tunnels.

The Word followed the long main tunnel until she saw a row of doors. Words were lining up outside them, waiting to be let in. The Word stood in the queue and waited her turn. When she produced her ticket, a very polite word personally escorted her from the entrance to her seat in the hall where the Linguistic Games were to take place.

The hall was vast. The Word was seated in a soft leather armchair, with a candle burning in front of it. But the candle by her seat wasn't the only one in the hall. A thousand lights danced in front of her eyes. She remembered the streams of words coursing through the city towards the central square. There was enough space for all those words here, and yet many of the seats were still empty. The hall resembled an amphitheatre. The front rows were made up of armchairs which were roomier than the more basic seating in the upper tiers, but all the seats had one thing in common – they all had a candle burning in front of them.

The Word made herself comfortable, closed her eyes and let the warmth of the candles wash over her as she waited for the Games to begin.

CHAPTER
SEVEN

The Linguistic Games

S

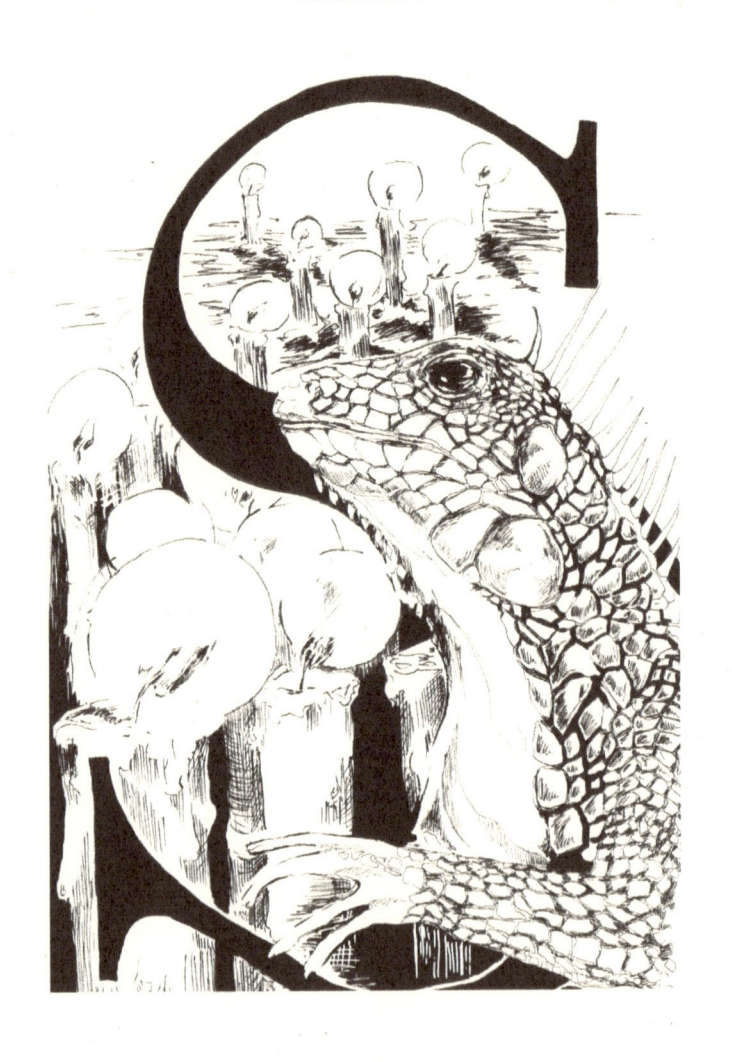

Soft rustling. The sound of pages turning. The Word opened her eyes. The candles in the auditorium had gone out. She saw the silhouettes of other words around her, all with their eyes fixed on the stage. A single candle burned there. In its light stood a word whose head was covered in reddish-brown scales. It was the lizard.

"*Wordsmith*," whispered a voice beside her.

For a moment the hall was filled with excited murmurs. The lizard waited for silence, then said, "Every word knows a story. Tales from days gone by. Adventures from our own lives. Made-up fairy tales, anecdotes and legends." As he spoke, he slowly paced up and down in the pool of candlelight. "Storytellers travel the world in search of a story worth telling, and when they find it, they bring it here to Langwich." The lizard paused for a moment. The tension in the auditorium was palpable. "Dear words, my name is Wordsmith, and I am delighted to welcome you to the Linguistic Games here in Langwich!"

The hall erupted into a thunderous chant: "Play! Play!"

Wordsmith left the stage, and a camel stepped into the candlelight. She bent her thin front legs awkwardly into a position resembling a bow.

"*The Black Desert*," said the camel in a sandy voice. "Words who lived in its foothills called it the 'Black Desert'. They did not give it that name because of its colour. True, it was black, as black as the graphite it was made of, but that was not the reason. Any word who dared set foot in the Black Desert was never seen again. It was called the Black Desert because it was seen as the bringer of death.

Despite its forbidding name, over the years many fearless words set out to cross the Black Desert. Legend had it that at the heart of the desert lay a palace of ivory. In the palace, so the story went, lived a venerable word, a king without a queen, who collected answers to his most pressing questions: what was the reason for his life? The reason for his wealth? The reason for his whole kingdom? Whenever anyone brought him an answer, they were rewarded by the king and lived out the rest of their days in abundance." The camel let her gaze wander over the audience.

"The legend was in fact true. Gathered together in the courtyard of the palace were *Pleasure, Selflessness, Justice, Knowledge, Permanence, Prosperity* and *Immortality*: answers brought by the words who had succeeded in reaching the palace. As the years went by, however, the legend of the palace in the desert sank into oblivion. Whenever a word arrived in the kingdom, it was showered with gifts and remained at the king's court for the rest of its life. No word ever returned from the desert to tell the tale, which might have rekindled the adventurous spirit of other words. Thus fewer and fewer words answered the call of the desert, and sometimes years went by before the king was brought a new answer. This made him uneasy. His collection had stopped growing, and yet he suspected that he still did not possess the truest answer of all. He commanded his serving words to saddle the pack animals and summon the bravest words to be found at his court. His caravan then set out to cross the black graphite dunes and rescue any word that had gone astray in the leaden dune fields. The king rode at the head of the procession on his camel – his 'ship of the desert', as the words called it. They journeyed for weeks and months, before finally coming across a lost word. Then the king brought *Godliness* home with him as well as *Nihilism*. When he returned from one of his expeditions, he was placated. He rewarded the traveller who had brought him the new answer, saw to the business of his court, and made any decisions that had been left unmade during his absence. This state of affairs lasted a few weeks, until the king began to have fresh doubts and once again started asking 'why'. Why was he alive? Why was he the king of this kingdom? There must be an answer out there truer than any of the answers he had found so far.

In this way the years passed, and the king never took a wife. He was always travelling, and all he ever thought about were the answers he still wanted to collect. The king journeyed to ever more distant parts of the Black Desert. Once the caravan travelled for months without coming across a new word. And after a whole year had passed without success, the king began to doubt himself. He looked at the endless expanse of dark dunes stretching out before him, and felt lonelier than he had ever felt in his life. He thought about his court, which he had left to fend for itself. He thought about the many answers collected in his palace, which he hadn't seen for such a long time. And he thought of the queen he had never had. How could he have believed he would go on finding ever more truthful answers? Couldn't he be satisfied with what the desert had already given him? The king thought hard for many days, until at last he decided to return home. He wondered how his courtiers would react when he turned up without a new answer for his collection. Would they be disappointed in him? A few times he turned the caravan around again, wanting to continue his search, but each time he thought better of it and turned back.

After an absence of almost two years, when the caravan returned to the palace, the whole court assembled to greet it.

They cheered the king and his companions, whom they had believed to be lost. When the king dismounted his camel, they had to turn their faces away until their eyes had adjusted to the beautiful word sitting behind him on the saddle. On the journey home, the king had found *Wisdom*, his future queen, who showed him that what really mattered was not knowing all the answers in the world, but finding his own happiness. And so they lived together in the Black Desert happily ever after."

The camel bowed awkwardly once more and left the stage amid rapturous applause. The Word was impressed, and wondered whether the camel was the same one the king had ridden across the Black Desert. Wordsmith returned to the stage. He too was clapping.

"Excellent! Truly excellent," he said, as the applause gradually died down. "Dear words, we now come to the scoring."

Suddenly the candle in front of the Word's seat flickered into life, as did all the other candles in the hall.

"You will find your seat candle directly in front of you. When you hear the pages rustle, you must make your decision. If you enjoyed the camel's story, leave your candle burning. Otherwise, blow it out."

The sound of rustling pages was heard, and the Word knew at once that she was going to leave her candle burning. How could she possibly blow it out when the story had been told so beautifully? But some of the words did extinguish their candles. On one side of the stage, a number mounted the steps. It called out: "82!" and then left the stage.

"82 points out of 100 for the camel!" said Wordsmith.

The candles in front of the words' seats went out again. Only the candle on the stage was left alight.

Storyteller after storyteller vied for the audience's votes. The Word thought all the stories were extraordinary, full of depth and imagination. She marvelled at them as she leaned back in her chair and listened. Some of the stories made her sad, some scared her, and a few were so beautiful and moving that they brought tears to her eyes. After every story came the sound of rustling pages. The Word never blew out her candle. Who was she to judge the quality of the stories being told? There were some she didn't understand at all, until their meaning was suddenly revealed in the final wordlet. And perhaps it was exactly the same in her own case as well, she thought. Perhaps she just had to wait for her story to end in order to understand her own meaning and the meaning of all the adventures she'd had. Other storytellers painted the most amusing pictures in her mind's eye. She saw a slippery salesman who had lost all his customers because nobody could ever get hold of him, and a house that was so haunted it scared away its own ghosts. And then there were some really wacky yarns: a fairy tale about two snails who started out infinitely far apart but who, undeterred, ventured slowly towards each other in the hope of meeting at a singularity; stories about enchanted frogs and magic mirrors and talking clocks and lovesick letters. All the stories had one thing in common, however: they were all fantastical. They were narrated from an unusual perspective as if they wanted to show familiar things in a new light.

Slowly the Linguistic Games neared their conclusion. The audience had selected five storytellers, each of whom told one more story until eventually only two competitors remained. Wordsmith stepped onto the stage. The candle cast a reddish-gold light over his scaly face.

"Dear words, it is time. The finalists of the Linguistics have been selected!"

The crowd applauded.

"Come on to the stage and reveal yourselves!"

Two storytellers stepped onto the stage. The camel had made it to the final. Apart from the story about the desert, she had also told an entertaining tale about a transformational leader who tried to turn lead into gold. Alongside the camel, an elegant word came onto the stage. He was holding a thick book in his hands. His stories had been especially good, thought the Word. One of them had been about a historian who climbed a family tree in search of his ancestors and couldn't get down again. Another story had been about a little prince who saw things you can only see with the heart.

"*Just* will begin," said Wordsmith, and left the stage.

All eyes turned to the man who was now standing on stage all alone. In a voice as clear as glass, he uttered the title: "*Just*." His story has the same name as him, thought the Word, intrigued, and settled down to listen.

"I grew up in an orphanage. One of my first memories is of a large hall, where I am playing with the other children. In a corner I have built a wall out of building blocks, and I am hiding behind it. I can't remember my parents – I was much too young when they died.

When I was older, I no longer hid behind walls but behind empty phrases. When one of the guardians asked me what I wanted to do, I would reply shyly, 'I'd be happy just not causing a bother.'

If one of the other children came up to me and asked if I wanted to be friends, I would answer bashfully: 'I'm just a simple word. What do you want with me?'

I grew even older and dreamed of seeing the world – I just felt too scared to leave the orphanage. I wanted to learn new languages but I didn't dare speak the foreign wordlets out loud."

Just paused for a moment and gazed, lost in thought, into the flame of the burning candle before him. Then he looked back at the audience.

"In the orphanage, there was a little reading room I used to retreat to. I didn't know what to expect from my life. I wanted to be a word of honour, married with children and a job that would enable me to provide for my family. But I wasn't sure this path was open to me. I was just a short word without a past, without a family. What could possibly become of me? In books, however, it was different. There, it was orphans who did things they never would have thought possible and had the most perilous adventures. Beggars found treasure in enchanted places that everyone else had stopped believing in. And in books, the boy who nobody ever paid any attention to would be the one to win the princess's heart, despite his crooked nose and sagging shoulders – because a magic spell would help her see past his outward appearance and into his soul, where she found nothing but beauty. I hid myself in these stories and read everything the little reading room had to offer. Once I'd read most of the books, I would wait impatiently for the monthly donations that came in from the city, in the hope that amongst the clothes and food parcels there might also be some new books. But it wasn't just adventure stories I read. I also devoured crime novels and romances, poetry and non-fiction – anything that came in the monthly donated bundles and found its way to the reading room. The books had become my refuge, and the more I read, the more erudite I became. Gradually, the world opened up to me. I suddenly understood things that remained hidden to other words. At first, it was just the children in the orphanage who came to me. Although I'd never seen the sea before, I was able to explain the tides to them. And though we'd only ever seen snow in picture books, I was able to explain to them why water was transparent but snow was white. That was just the younger children, however. The older ones came to me because they sought my advice. They often wanted to ask me about quarrels, jealousy, disappointment or unrequited love. Nothing I hadn't already read about in a book. I always said, 'I'm just a short word, but if you ask me, I'd say …'

It wasn't long before my reputation for being able to help people with their disagreements spread to the world outside the orphanage. Two words from the city came to see me – *Violin* and *Silence*. They were neighbours, and firmly at loggerheads. As they sat there in front of me, neither of them made a sound. They sat silently side by side, but I wasn't too worried about that. Sometimes these things take time. Then Violin exclaimed, 'Look at him sitting there in silence. He's actually enjoying it! Instead of talking about the problem.' Silence said nothing, and Violin went on, 'I have to practise, don't I? He complains that I'm always making noise and he can't hear himself think, whatever that's supposed to mean. What should I do?'

I explained to them what I'd read in a book: 'I'm just a short word, but if you ask me, every word in this world has its counterword: a word with exactly the opposite meaning. Only through its counterword does a word acquire its own meaning – no love without hate, no warmth without coldness, no nearness without distance. It's like in an orchestra. The violin needs the double bass and the double bass needs the violin. Otherwise the concert won't sound as good. But it's important to get the timing right. That's why you two should consider yourselves lucky to be neighbours. Silence requires noise, and noise silence. You just have to find the right timing for both of you.' Violin understood, and promised to play only during the daytime. Silence remained silent, content.

More and more words came to see me and asked for my advice. But no matter how much advice I gave, I still couldn't answer the gnawing question about my own life. What was going to become of me?

Then one day, a monarch butterfly came to the orphanage with his beautiful fiancée, a ladybird. The managers of the orphanage were all aflutter. The monarch was a member of the royal family, and the ladybird was the mayor's daughter.

These were the most illustrious personages to set foot in the orphanage since its opening. The monarch brought gifts: stonemasons and carpenters to re-plaster the flaking walls and replace the roof beams, which had begun to rot over the decades. The monarch didn't stop to talk to the managers for long. He was looking for the word that gave such good advice.

Just a short while later, I found myself face-to-face with the monarch butterfly and his fiancée, in their reddish-orange wing robes. As I shut the reading room door behind us, someone whispered to me from outside, 'Advise him well. The orphanage needs a benefactor like him.'

I greeted them both and invited them to sit down. One glance from the monarch was enough to prompt his fiancée to begin the conversation. The ladybird started to explain: 'The monarch is too stubborn. Whenever I do something that displeases him, he gets angry and orders me about as if I were one of his servants. We've been engaged for half a year now. I see this as a trial period.'

The red of his wings shone more vividly as the monarch replied, 'The lady thinks you might be able to give her some advice about how she could handle the situation better.'

'How I could handle the situation better?' his fiancée exclaimed. 'I think it's the monarch who needs advice about how he should handle such situations.'

'We've heard enough. Let the little word speak now, and let's put this to bed. Please.' The monarch pointed to me and fell silent.

I thought about the crumbling plaster on the orphanage walls and the monthly donations we all relied upon. I knew what the monarch wanted to hear. I was supposed to explain to his fiancée that a successful man has to give orders, and she should count herself lucky to be engaged to a man as successful as him. But that wouldn't have been the truth. So instead, I told him, 'I'm just a short word, and I don't know much about it, but if you ask me, you have to make compromises in a relationship, just as you do in a democracy. If the lady does something the monarch doesn't like, then you ought to talk to each other about it. As equals. Perhaps there's a good reason why the lady is doing it that way. In such situations, getting angry and trying to give orders doesn't help.'

'Democracy?' The monarch's wings were now blood-red. 'I've never heard anything so ridiculous in all my life. What does a sneaky little word like you know about democracy? An orphan, abandoned by his own parents!'

'Stop insulting him this instant. You know who he is,' the ladybird sprang to my defence.

'I'll show you what I think of democracy.' He spread his splendid wings menacingly. 'This orphanage will not be visited by any members of the royal family for another hundred years! There will be no restoration work, and the monthly donations will be halved!'

'If you do that, I'll leave you!' cried the ladybird.

'Then leave me,' the monarch retorted, and he threw open the doors of the reading room and stormed out.

I felt terrible. 'I'm so sorry,' I apologised, 'I'm just a simple short word. I'm so stupid, I've done everything wrong.'

'No, no. It's quite alright. I would have left him anyway, sooner or later. Better now, like this, than when it would be too late,' the ladybird tried to reassure me.

'Why did you come to see me in the first place? I'm just an

insignificant word. I just don't know how I could have been so forward as to tell him the truth.'

'You're not just an insignificant word, you're not just Just,' she broke in. 'I know your parents' story. You're like them: honest, principled, impartial. You're already what many others want to be but never will be: a word of honour. You are just. And you must be careful, because you may pay for it with your life. Just like your parents.'

'My parents?' I asked incredulously. 'What do you know about my parents?'

'You come from an honourable family. Your father was the city magistrate, and your mother was a justice of the peace. My father admired your parents: they stood up for the vulnerable, and always abided by the same guiding principle – the truth. They were impartial and incorruptible. That's why so many words come to see you. They know you're the same. Sadly, your parents paid for it with their lives. My father tried to save them, but in vain. He was the one who brought you to this orphanage. He wanted to protect you, even if he couldn't save your parents. Nobody was supposed to know who you are.'"

Just bowed. When the sound of rustling pages began, the Word left her candle burning. The number hoisted itself onto the stage again. "69!" it called.

Wordsmith returned to the stage. "69 points for the story of how the insignificant Just became a word of honour. Thank you very much."

Next the camel stepped forward, bowed and began: "Once I was travelling in the deserts of the Orient. Beneath the blazing sun, sitting alone in that vast expanse of sand, I came across a melancholy storyteller. He told me that some time ago, having stopped at an oasis, he'd told his thousandth tale. His audience had thought very highly of it. They'd given him fruit and water, enough for his onward journey. But now he couldn't think of any more stories, and his provisions were running out. He didn't dare set foot in the next oasis without a new tale to regale people with. What if there was a word in the audience he'd already met, who already knew his stories?

I stayed with the poor storyteller and shared my bread and water with him. When night fell and the stars came out in the clear desert sky, I decided to give the downcast word one of my stories as a gift. I told him the title of the story – *The Nesting Doll* – and then I began:

| 'When you're young, life is wonderfully exciting. Almost everywhere you go, you stumble across stories in which you could be the main character, if you wanted to be. Every story is a unique miracle. But when children stumble across a miracle, they get straight back up again, because they know that if they just lay there, they'll miss out on all kinds of other miracles. Miracles are different when you're a child. They're smaller and so much simpler. But if you're lucky, even as an adult you can still come across one. A miracle takes the form of a fairy tale that seems so fantastical you don't know where the fairy tale ends and your own life begins. Miracles like that don't come along very often – sometimes not at all, or only in small morsels. But when you're young, oh, my goodness! I tell you, you can barely move for miracles. Let me tell you a story:

|| Once upon a time there was a little girl named Sophie. Because Sophie was still a child, she loved stumbling across miracles, and she was very good at it – so good that by rights

she ought to have been covered in bruises, except that miracles don't leave bruises, only precious memories. Sophie also had a brother, who doesn't play a particularly important role in this story. I only mention him because he helps explain a particular quirk of Sophie's character. Sophie was the only one who possessed this trait – her brother didn't have the slightest trace of it. Sophie was a girl who loved stories more than anything else in the world. In every word she saw, she recognised the hidden story behind it. That little grain of a story which she saw in every word made Sophie love all words, even the ones that are loved by hardly anybody else. She was enchanted by the world and went dancing through it, singing it her most beautiful songs.

One day, it so happened that she and her brother were sitting in the shade of a tree, and a snake was coiled around a branch in the treetop. When the snake saw the two children, it came slithering down the trunk of the tree.

'Psst,' said the snake.

The boy started up and ran away and left his sister there all alone. But Sophie put out her hand to the snake, which wound itself around her fingers, then her arm, and finally her whole body. Only Sophie's head was still visible. She looked into the snake's face without fear.

'Psst,' said the snake.

'Yes?' asked Sophie.

'I want to tell you a story.'

'I'd like that,' said Sophie. So the snake began:

||| 'Once upon a time, many years ago, there was a little girl. This little girl loved playing outdoors. She would spend hours and hours frolicking in the fresh air, happily whiling the days away. The great outdoors was so full of new things

to discover that she never got bored. One afternoon, she went out as usual in search of something to discover – and lo and behold, she was in luck. After walking along, looking around and waiting awhile, and then walking along again, all of a sudden something stopped her in her tracks. A long time stood before her. The time was so long that it towered above the little girl, being several times her height.

"Good day," she said to the time.

"Good day my foot," spat the time. "It's a terrible day!"

"But why is it a terrible day?" she asked.

"It's not just today – all my days are terrible, and they're getting terribler and terribler."

"But why?" asked the girl.

"Because every day I get shorter, and one day I'll run out altogether," the time answered.

"But you're still very long," reasoned the girl, trying to console the time.

"Yes," it said, "I still seem long to you, but just you wait a few years – then I won't seem long at all anymore."

"I don't understand," the girl replied.

"I'll tell you a story," said the time, and began:

|||| *"Once upon a time, many years ago, there was a little girl. Her name was Sophie. Sophie had a brother whom she loved very much. But there were many other things she loved, too: in fact, she loved almost everything in the world, and above all else she loved stories. One day, the two children were sitting in the shade of a tree where a snake was lying lazily in the branches. When it saw the children, it came slithering down towards them. On seeing the snake, Sophie's brother started up and ran away, leaving his sister all alone. Sophie wasn't scared though. She put out her hand to the snake and*

let it wrap itself around her body. The snake said it wanted to tell Sophie a story, and since Sophie loved stories above all things, she listened avidly.

Thus the years passed, and the snake talked on and on but somehow the story never came to an end. Sophie was getting older, although she didn't realise it. The snake had wrapped itself around her body so she couldn't see that she was gradually ageing. When the snake finally reached the end of its story, it also reached the end of its life. It died, decayed and fell away.

Finally Sophie could see her body again, and it shocked her, for only now did she realise how much she had aged. She got to her feet with difficulty and walked very slowly to a nearby lake. She leaned over the surface of the water and looked into the face of the old woman she had become. Then Sophie said to herself, 'Once, a long time stood before me. I never even thought about getting old. But now all my time has run out.'

Sophie looked into her own eyes reflected in the lake, and searched for that little grain she was accustomed to finding in everything, which made her love everything no matter what it was. And now she searched for that grain in herself, the little story inside herself that she could love, no matter how old she got. After a while she found the grain in her eye, and it said, 'I'd like to tell you a story.'

Sophie wasn't sure she wanted to hear another story. She felt as though the snake had already told her every story that could possibly exist in the world.

'Is it a long story?' she asked. 'I don't have a great deal of time, you see.'

The grain stared back at her for a while and then disappeared forever. Just before it vanished, Sophie heard it whisper:

'Yes.'"

The time had come to the end of its story. ||||

"What happened to Sophie?" asked the little girl.

The time, which already seemed a little shorter, looked down at the girl. "Sophie had stopped loving stories. The snake's story had been so long that she didn't feel it was worth listening to any more stories. She didn't even care about her own story. In the end, her time ran out, and she died a few days later."

"That's a sad story," said the girl to the time,' said the snake, concluding its story. |||

Sophie was astonished. How could it be that she and the snake featured in the story that the snake itself was telling?

'Have I really been listening to your story for such a long time?' Sophie asked the snake. She was puzzled to see that the snake was still alive, even though its story had come to an end.

'No, this story was a lot shorter than the one I told you in my story,' the snake replied. It uncoiled itself, and Sophie could see her own body again – she was no older than she had been before.

'Then why did you tell the story that way?' Sophie asked.

The snake replied, 'I wanted to show you that you need to go through life a little more cautiously. Often in this world we come across a story that threatens to trap us, and whenever that happens, we must ensure that diving into this story is really the right thing to do. We are not given much time in this life, and there are so many stories we could choose to pursue. We must think very carefully about which story is worth spending our life with.'

And so you see how fairy tales can suddenly become part of our own lives. Whenever we come across such a fairy tale in life, the miracle is not far behind. All we need to do is open our eyes.'

The storyteller thanked me for the story I had given him. He didn't want to call it *The Nesting Doll* anymore. From now on he would call it *The Tale from One Thousand and One Nights*, and many more stories would follow this one." With this, the camel ended her story.

She waited impassively for the audience's reaction. At first there was silence. Then Just began to clap his hands. Other words joined in the applause and clapped louder than they had all evening. The Word herself had enjoyed the story immensely. Both the titles were well chosen, she thought, for the story really was like a nesting doll, with several stories nestled one inside the other, waiting for their meanings to be unfurled. The Word was moved. She wasn't sure she'd understood everything the snake had said, but she felt as though the parts she did grasp had been just for her. Wordsmith appeared on the stage. He was clapping his scaly hands too.

"Thank you, thank you very much," he said.

The sound of rustling pages filled the air. The candles by the words' seats flickered into life. The Word left her candle alight, and looked around the hall. The odd flame was snuffed out here and there, but most of the words left theirs burning. The number returned to the stage.

"92!" it cried.

"92 points for the camel," said Wordsmith.

The camel looked delightedly around the hall and bowed once more.

"And now, before we move on to the award ceremony, we come to an old tradition with which the Games will close this year as they do every year," Wordsmith announced. "The next time the pages rustle, all the candles will go out, even up here on the stage. Only one candle in the hall will light up. The word whose candle it is will get the chance to come up onto the stage and tell their own story."

The Word felt uneasy. She hoped her candle wouldn't be the one that lit up. Then the rustling pages sounded, and the hall was plunged into darkness. Here and there a soft whispering could be heard, but the Word couldn't see a thing. She closed her eyes. She'd loved the Linguistic Games. She thought about the fantastical stories, about Sophie, the snake and the camel. And she marvelled at the fact that she'd met Wordsmith, of all words, back there in the tunnel. He was going to have a prime spot at the Games, he'd said. And here he was standing on the stage, hosting them! Then the rustling sounded again. The Word opened her eyes and froze. The candle in front of her seat was alight.

CHAPTER
EIGHT

The Word Joins In

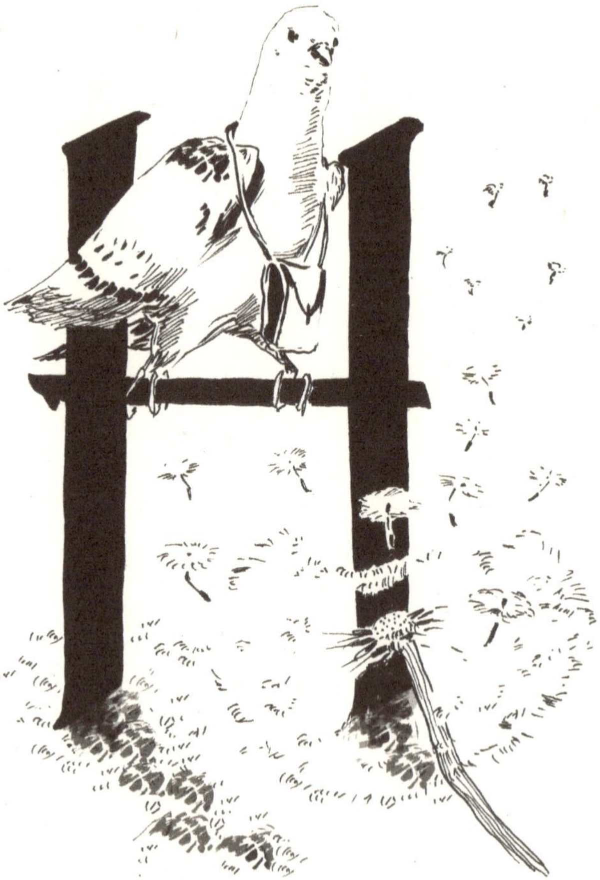

Her candle was alight. It was alight. It was *alight*! The thought echoed through her mind, paralyzing her. How could this be happening? Why her? Wordsmith had left the stage and come out into the auditorium, and now he was standing right in front of her.

"Do you know any stories?" he whispered so quietly that only she could hear him.

"No," she replied. "I don't even know my name. I've forgotten everything."

"Was it a human?" asked Wordsmith.

"Yes. I can't get up on that stage."

"Yes you can. Every word knows at least one story."

"I don't! Please choose someone else."

"No," said the lizard. "I owe it to you. We're going to go onstage, and you're going to tell us a story you didn't even know you had in you. Don't think of things you already know or things you've already experienced – those aren't what great stories are made of. Think of something new. Use your imagination. Then it won't matter a bit what you've forgotten." He drew her out of her seat. The audience's applause mingled with the pounding of her heart as she and Wordsmith walked together towards the stage.

The camel nodded kindly to the Word as she took her place in the pool of candlelight. Pages rustled: the signal for her to start her story. There was silence in the theatre now. The candle cast a warm light over her face. The Word closed her eyes. She must use her imagination, Wordsmith had said, and this immediately reminded her of Mad. Hadn't he said something similar? As long as she had imagination, she would also have meaning. But where was she supposed to find this imagination they kept telling her about? At first, she couldn't see anything. But then a handful of wordlets appeared before her, glowing brightly – *animal, flower, conversation, feeling, desire*. She didn't know where the wordlets had come from, but she sensed that they were the key to her story and could open the door to her imagination. Suddenly she opened her mouth and spoke, surprising herself more than anyone else in the theatre.

"*The Carrier Pigeon*," she titled her story.

She felt like telling a fantastical story, and now yet another wordlet appeared before her mind's eye – *fly*. So she began:

"'I want to fly!' sighed the flower. 'I want to fly so badly, on an eagle's back or a genie's magic carpet. I want to flap my leaves up and down so quickly that I rise into the sky!'

A carrier pigeon heard her, fluttered to the ground and drew out one of the countless little slips of paper she carried in her leather satchel. It read: 'Why do you want to fly?'

'Because the dandelions told me how wonderful it is,' the flower replied.

The pigeon looked at the flower. Her stem was slightly bent, with thick, narrow leaves. Her bud drooped disappointedly. The pigeon plucked another slip of paper from her bag. 'What sort of flower are you?' it read.

'I don't know. I don't have a name,' she replied, then added, 'Can you help me?'

The pigeon gave her a slip of paper. 'I wish I could give you my wordlet that you too will fly one day.'

'Why can't you?' asked the flower.

This time the message was a little longer. 'When I was young, I carelessly gave my wordlet to too many acquaintances. In the end I simply didn't have any wordlets left. And so I became mute. All I had left were my letters.'

The flower appreciated the pigeon's honesty. You shouldn't make promises lightly – in fact, you should really only make a promise if you are sure you can keep it. But as long as you are able to admit to your own mistakes, you can be sure to grow and improve.

The flower and the pigeon became friends. Every day the pigeon brought at least one letter. In it, she wrote to the flower about what it was like to fly and what she had seen on her journeys. In return, the flower taught the pigeon how to turn her wings towards the sun after a rain shower to dry them quicker. At the same time, she felt sorry for the pigeon. Being mute, she felt, was too harsh a punishment for a few broken promises."

The Word couldn't help thinking of the promise she'd made to Rhyme and Reason. Would she ever manage to find her way back to them, to see the finished statue? She had lost control of her story. Just as the words in the audience were listening to her, she too listened to herself. Somewhere in the depths of her mind, she sensed where the story might go, but she didn't know whether it would ever actually reach its destination. All the threads had to be brought together, all the loose ends tied up. Excited to hear what she was going to say next, she carried on.

"The closer it got to summer, the better the flower felt. The warmth enveloped her deliciously, and the late spring breeze tingled on her leaves. Slowly she bloomed and revealed petals as white as the letters the pigeon wrote for her. The flower had kept the letters secretly tucked away in her enclosed blossoms. Now black letters fell from her blossoms like seeds upon the ground. The pigeon flew down and gave the flower another slip of paper: 'Your bloom is beautiful!'"

The Word cried out the pigeon's words to the audience in the hall. By this time, she had forgotten she was at the Linguistic Games. She was completely immersed in her story, connecting what she had already told with what was yet to come.

"The flower blushed, and her white petals were suffused with pink. 'The seeds are for you,' she said.

The pigeon pecked them up one by one and immediately felt a change. She cleared her throat and spoke for the first time in many years. 'This is the nicest present anyone has ever given me,' she exclaimed. 'From now on, I will call you *letterdrop*, and wherever I fly, your seeds will fly with me like those of a dandelion.'"

The Word came to the end of her story and enjoyed the moment of silence. She felt that even if she'd wanted to go on telling the story, she wouldn't have been able to. It had chosen its own ending. The Word couldn't help thinking of the story the camel had told about Sophie, the snake and the time. *Sometimes you encounter a miracle which takes the form of a fairy tale – one that seems so fantastical you don't know where the fairy tale ends and your own life begins. Then you have to make sure that diving into this story is really the right thing to do.* She'd thought the camel was talking about life, which was akin to the telling of a long tale, assigning a different story to every word. But now she'd understood the second meaning too. The Word had been completely immersed in the wordlets she'd spoken, oblivious to everything but the flower and the pigeon conversing. The story, for the short time she'd been telling it, had become her life. Maybe there were stories like that too, she thought. And then the moment passed, and sound returned. The Word could hear the rustling, and low whispers from the audience. Nobody was clapping. It was as if the words were waiting for someone to tell them what to do next. Wordsmith stood there without moving, looking at the Word. Then he broke the uneasy silence, and declared, "A lovely story."

The camel was the first word to put its hooves together to make a sound vaguely resembling a clap. Gradually other words joined in, until lukewarm applause could be heard all over the auditorium.

The sound of rustling pages was followed by candles being lit up in the hall, although many of them were blown out again immediately. The number, pulling itself up onto the stage, called out: "25!"

Wordsmith thanked the Word and led her back to her seat. "Wait here for me until the Games are over," he whispered.

Then came the awards ceremony, at which the camel was presented with the golden laurel wreath of the city of Langwich. Once the camel had obliged the audience with a short encore – another story about the desert – Wordsmith declared the Games officially over. The candles in the hall were lit again, and the words began to filter out of the auditorium.

"More of them should have left their candles lit," said the lizard. The Word sat silently beside him in the now empty theatre. "Your story was good."

"Then why did the words blow their candles out?" she asked.

"They couldn't understand how a word who's never competed at the Linguistics before could possibly come out with a story like that. They were expecting an anecdote from your childhood, or some well-worn fairy tale they'd all heard a hundred times before. Your story was new! There are many words for whom the quality of a story is not the most important thing. To them, all that matters is who's telling the story. It has to be one of those terribly important words who are oh-so profound and full of meaning. *Audacity. Superiority. Mastery.* They couldn't stand to see an insignificant word win the Games. The camel they could accept. The ship of the desert. A nice metaphor. But you? What do you stand for?"

The Word ignored the question. "It was strange," she said thoughtfully. "When I stepped onto the stage with you, I had no idea what I was going to say. I tried to do what you said – I tried to find the imagination inside me. Suddenly wordlets just appeared before my eyes, and the story told itself."

"That's exactly how it is," Wordsmith replied. "As a storyteller, you have to keep searching for imagination. You have to search for it anew every time you tell a story. Sometimes you find it straight away, but often the search takes a very long time. Then you go through an agonising wait – hours, days, weeks, or in my case, years."

"Years?" the Word asked.

"Most words in the world of language know who I am. Perhaps you once knew me too, before you were spoken out loud. When I was young, I won the Linguistics three times in a row. No word had ever done that before. I just stepped onto the stage and told my stories without needing to prepare. The wordlets simply came to me when I needed them. The door to my imagination was wide open. That's how it was for a good few years, until one day I started finding it harder and harder to tell stories. I began borrowing bits of old stories to use in my new ones. Nobody noticed. But when it became clear to me that I was getting fewer and fewer ideas, I decided to stop competing. I didn't want to deceive my audience. For years I collected ideas, until I had enough to be able to return to the stage. Then, in one evening, I used up all the ideas I'd worked so hard to accumulate. The feeling of being onstage again was indescribable. But afterwards I felt hollow and used up – an empty word, fit for nothing."

"So you're still collecting ideas?" asked the Word.

"No. I've given up storytelling for good. My only role at the Linguistics these days is as the host. Believe it or not, I've found something that feels just as good as standing on stage and telling stories."

"What's that?"

Wordsmith looked at the Word intently, hesitated for a moment and then said, "I can show you. Tomorrow. But I can't tell you what it is, because then you wouldn't agree to come with me. You have to be brave to do this, you more than any other word. And you have to trust me."

The Word met the lizard's eye. Surprised by the earnestness of his words, she replied, "I trust you."

For a long while they carried on talking. Wordsmith told her about his past, about the stories he'd told and the victories he'd achieved. Neither of them mentioned what he planned to show her the next day. The candles in the theatre burned low, until darkness engulfed the two words. And then, dreaming of the fantastic stories she'd heard at the great Linguistic Games, the Word fell into a deep, sound sleep.

CHAPTER
NINE

A Winged Word

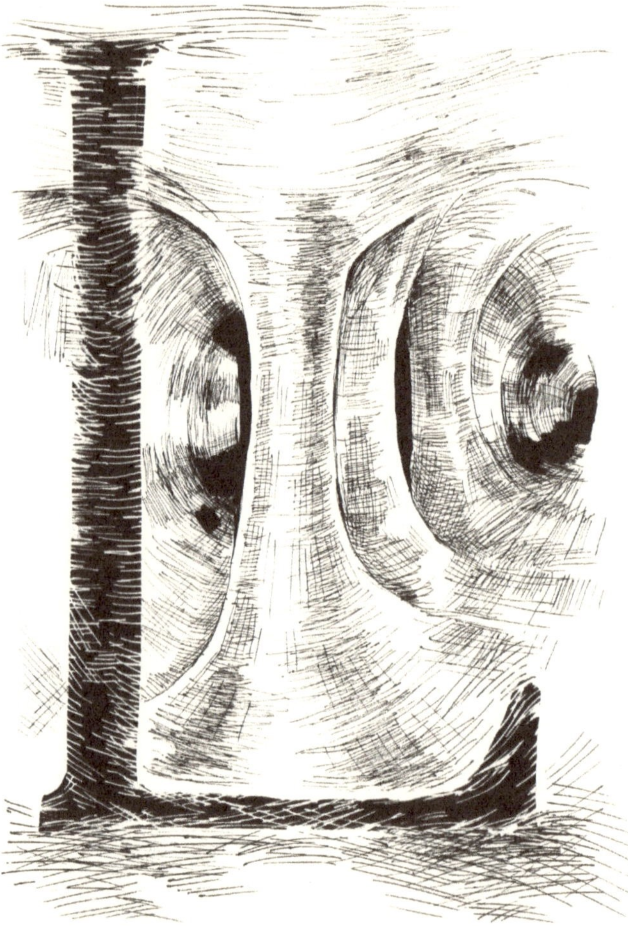

"Let's go."

The Word opened her eyes. For a moment she couldn't work out who was speaking. Then she recognised the lizard. "If we get there too late, I won't be able to find the exit. But there should still be enough light outside if we leave now," urged Wordsmith.

The main tunnel was well lit, but soon they branched off into narrower tunnels illuminated only by a few solitary candles.

"The tunnels form a network beneath the city. You can travel quickly from place to place. It's said they were originally built as escape tunnels, for words fleeing from humans. There are hardly any words who know their way around down here anymore. Many of the tunnels are unlit and some of them lead right out of the city."

The Word said nothing, just nodded. She kept being reminded of her encounter with the grey bird.

"The last candle." Wordsmith took it down from the wall and strode on into the darkness. The tunnel they were walking down was a long one, and it seemed to the Word to grow narrower with every step they took.

"How do you know your way around the tunnels so well?" she asked.

"When I was still competing in the Linguistics, I went looking everywhere for ideas to use in my stories. The old tunnel system was perfect. Plenty of inspiration for adventure stories and saturnine tales. The most intriguing tunnels were the pitch-black ones; nobody knew quite where they led."

The lizard paused. Right in front of them, a hole had been bored at the bottom of the rocky wall. Wordsmith pointed to it. "From now on we'll have to go on our hands and knees. And we won't be able to take the candle. Stay close behind me." He extinguished the candle flame and squeezed into the narrow passageway. The Word followed him. It was difficult to navigate the tunnel in such thick darkness. Loose stones lay on the ground, digging painfully into her letters. She crawled slowly onwards. After a while, Wordsmith came to a halt.

"Here it is," he said. "Directly above us is the shaft that leads to the exit. Do you see the light filtering in?"

"No, I can't see anything at all."

"Yes you can. Look hard and you'll see it. It's a little bit lighter than before."

The Word imagined for an instant that she could see the lizard's silhouette, but the impression faded again a moment later.

"What now?" she asked.

"I'll go up first. When I get near the top, you climb up after me. You'll have to manage the first part alone. Wedge yourself in between the walls and work your way upwards."

"What will I find up there?"

The lizard was silent for a moment. Then he replied: "Not everything is black and white. There are shades of grey. Trust me."

The Word climbed into the narrow shaft and inched her way upwards. Wordsmith was right, thought the Word, it was starting to get brighter. Through the lizard's legs she could see the opening at the surface from where the light was entering. At the top, Wordsmith climbed out, then reached back down into the hole and pulled her up the rest of the way. At long last she felt solid ground beneath her feet again.

They were standing in a meadow. Nearby were about twenty other words, holding hands in pairs and ... dancing. The words spun around, let go of each other, found new partners and carried on dancing. There was no music to be heard, but all the words were moving perfectly in sync with one another.

"It'll be our turn soon," said Wordsmith, pointing upwards to where a little bird with metallic green feathers was fluttering in the air. His long, pointed beak was as blue as his gleaming throat, and his wings beat so fast that they seemed transparent. His black eyes gazed down at the Word and the lizard.

The Word felt warmth spreading through her body, and a thudding in her chest. Bom. Bom-bom. Bom. Bom-bom. Her heart was beating to the rhythm of the bird's fluttering wings. She was overcome by an urge to start dancing, and began to move in time with the wingbeats. Hands clasped hers, then let go again. Now and then she found herself partnered with Wordsmith, dancing a few steps with him, and then moving on to the next word. It was as if someone was guiding her steps. All she had to do was let go and allow the energy of the movement to take over. The group was now moving towards a little hill on the other side of the valley. Somewhere in the Word's mind, a memory stirred. She couldn't take her eyes off the hill. She'd seen this sight once before. She recognised those things up there on the hill and she knew what they were, those two straight-backed creatures towering above them. They were vocal cords! If she didn't do something soon, she and the other words would all be doomed.

"Run!" she cried, abruptly letting go of her unsuspecting

dance partner, who lost his balance and fell over forwards. A few words faltered and went off time, but quickly regained the rhythm and went on dancing as if nothing had happened. "Run, please, run!" cried the Word. When she realised none of the other words were listening, she fought her way out of the group and turned back towards the tunnel, ready to flee. At that moment, however, the little bird came fluttering down from the sky and hovered in the air in front of her. The Word stood still. The bird's black eyes were trained on her. She wanted to run away, but her body no longer obeyed her. The little bird had taken control of it. He guided her back into the group, just as he had guided her steps during the dance. Wordsmith was beside her. The vocal cords were looming above them now. And then the first few words leapt through the gap between the cords and disappeared. The lizard took the Word's hand.

"You don't need to be afraid," he said. Her eyes filled with tears when she saw the yawning chasm between the cords. Then she jumped too.

The Word awoke to the sounds of music. She was lying in a poppy field, gazing up at the clouds drifting overhead. Violins were playing, and the clouds were forming all kinds of shapes – one looked like a book, another a quill. There was a third cloud that looked just like Wordsmith. The Word felt herself being lifted off the ground. She heard the sound of bells and flutes. Suddenly she too was a cloud, floating through the air along with the book, the quill and Wordsmith. The music grew louder, and more clouds rose into the sky. Then the Word heard them singing – a polyphonic melody with silvery tones. Whenever a word sang its own name, a cloud disappeared from the sky. The Word felt that it was time for her to sing too. She opened her mouth and knew it was her own name that she sang. She couldn't make it out. All she could hear were the flutes and the violins and the music she was helping create. Then the cloud she had become began to break up, and eventually vanished.

The Word awoke and found herself back in the valley where she'd been just before jumping through the cords. She looked up at the bird hovering in the air above her, directing the dancing words with his wingbeats. The Word whispered to him, "Who are you?"

"Did you like it?" asked the bird.

"Who are you?"

"I am *Song*. Did you like it?"

"Yes," she said. "Very much. What was it?"

"You were sung," Song answered, glancing at the vocal cords.

"But how can that be?" asked the Word. "Why didn't it hurt? Why did it feel so nice?"

"When a human sings – really sings – they don't have to force words to reveal their names. The words come from the heart. They sing the names they carry within them quite naturally, of their own accord."

"What was that place I went to?" she asked.

"You were in a human's imagination. You saw exactly what he was seeing. Was it beautiful?"

"Yes, it was," she replied.

Even though the Word couldn't hear the music anymore, the song was still present somehow. The words in the valley twirled and looped, held each other's hands and let go again. It was a silent song, and their dancing filled the whole valley with it. The Word fell into step with them and let herself be guided by the little bird. Again she jumped through the opening between the two cords, and again she found herself in the human's imagination, became part of his song, reappeared and carried on dancing. As the sun touched the surrounding hills and the valley sank into red twilight, the Word suddenly stood still. The vocal cords had closed.

"Was it everything I promised?"

She turned and looked into Wordsmith's scaly face. Then she stepped forwards and embraced him. "It was wonderful!"

"I couldn't have told you before. I knew you carried the pain of having been spoken by a human."

"That's true. If you'd told me, I wouldn't have come."

Together they walked through the valley, which now lay in semi-darkness. Some of the words were sitting on the ground, talking quietly to one another, and others were leaning against each other dozing, or lying curled up in the grass fast asleep.

"Why have the vocal cords closed?" asked the Word.

"The human has stopped singing. All we can do is wait until the time is right again."

"How long will that take?"

"It can take several days. Humans are rather unpredictable," the lizard replied. "But it's been a long day – we should sleep now. Perhaps the cords will already be open again in the morning."

The Word bade the lizard goodnight, but she herself carried on walking through the valley for a while, thinking her own thoughts. She wondered who he was, this human who'd sung her. The hill on which the closed vocal cords stood was almost completely shrouded in darkness now. Only by the light of the moon could she see the little bird sitting in the grass at the foot of the hill. Song lifted his head and fixed his black eyes on her. Then he said: "In the past there were many vocal cords on this hill, all waiting for the right words."

"What happened?" the Word asked.

"We had to bid farewell to most of them. Humans have changed. They no longer have the patience to wait for the right words. They started to pressurise us, to give us meanings that didn't belong to us. They spoke us out loud when it would have been better to remain silent. And so words began to fear humans."

The Word listened intently to the little bird.

"When a human speaks you out loud at the right time, it's like magic. Their words gain a deeper meaning. Every word conceals a treasure within itself, and if you're spoken at the right moment, this treasure is revealed. But if a human speaks you at the wrong time, too late or too soon, or if they don't mean what they say, their words will have no meaning, and you may lose your meaning in the process. Have you ever felt you were speaking even though it wasn't the right moment to speak?"

"Yes," she answered.

"Take note of that feeling. Most words may not want to believe it, but we too need to make sure we don't speak wordlets out loud without reason."

When the Word returned to Wordsmith, he was already fast asleep. She would have liked to talk to someone else about Song, but she sensed that now was not the right moment to speak. And this time, thinking about the wordlets, she followed her instincts and stayed silent. After a moment she too lay down in the grass and fell into a deep, dreamless sleep.

"Are you awake?" asked a voice from beside her.

The Word was still groggy with sleep. She squinted through her half-closed eyes. Wordsmith was standing next to her, offering her his hand. She grabbed it and let him pull her to her feet. The first thing she did was look for the vocal cords. They were open. Words were already leaping through the gap between them. Song was fluttering in the air, guiding the words with his wingbeats.

"May I have this dance?" asked the lizard.

The Word's heart was pounding. Together, she and Wordsmith joined the group of dancing words and began to move to the rhythm of the bird's wingbeats. When they reached the hill where the vocal cords were standing, tall and straight-backed, the word no longer felt any fear. On the contrary, she was looking forward to diving into the human's imagination. What would she see this time? She sprang eagerly into the opening between the cords.

Time passed, and with every day that the Word spent in the valley she thought less and less about what her name was and what life had been like before she'd lost her memory. These anxieties had given way to contentment, a feeling of having found a place in the world which made her happy. She did not think about the future or the road that might lie ahead of her. She was happy now. And that was the only thing that mattered.

Without realising it, however, the Word had ended up in exactly the same situation the snake had warned Sophie about in the story at the Linguistic Games – she'd become embroiled in a story that threatened to trap her. The story of Song, which she was now part of, was getting longer and longer. And there were two things she was blissfully unaware of: the first was that with each day she spent dancing, she was moving further and further away from her true meaning, and the second thing, far more urgent, was that someone was already in the process of trying to change her story, which meant that she was in very grave danger indeed.

In another part of the world of language, the two creatures had crossed a river. The scent of the word they were tracking had gone cold. They hesitated for a moment, took each other's hands and conferred briefly. Then they set off again. They roamed the land for days without finding a trace of the word they were looking for. On a hill outside a grey city, they came to a halt. One of the creatures clawed a handful of earth out of the ground, and the other sniffed it. This was the scent they'd been created for. It was a senseless scent. Only a completely meaningless word could smell so overpoweringly of nothing. The creatures took each other's hands again. They seemed to be of one mind, for moments later they were on the move again. The brackets were back on the scent.

Somewhere in the valley, a figure slid out of a hole in the ground. It was night and almost everyone was asleep, so nobody saw it, or the second figure emerging shortly afterwards from the same hole. Only Song, in his flight over the valley, saw what was happening.

"Brackets!" he cried out in alarm, swooping down towards the two creatures. Again he screamed, "BRACKETS!"

The words awoke with a start, and fled when they saw the two creatures being divebombed by Song. He was trying to drive the brackets apart. He pecked at them with his sharp beak, and called, again and again: "Run! Run!" But his cries came too late for the Word. She stood frozen to the spot, desperately urging her syllables to move – but to no avail. One of the creatures was now standing right in front of her. Song circled above her head. "Go! Run!" The Word turned. The second bracket was behind her. They were closing in on her from both sides.

...

> The Word cried out in fear, but nobody could hear her screams anymore. The brackets had already taken each other's hands. They were standing so close together that their bodies had become walls. She was surrounded by whiteness so glaring that it burned. She closed her eyes and desperately beat her fists against the walls.

The two brackets set off. Wordsmith had leapt to his feet too. He realised far too late what had happened. He saw the little bird trying to peck at the brackets, who moved on obliviously, holding each other's hands as they travelled further and further away from the valley. The lizard was left behind.

The Word was deeply shaken. Trapped between the brackets, cut off from the world, she cried, "Let me out! Let me out of here!"

"Shouting won't get you anywhere … anywhere … anywhere …" came the reply, a clanging echo that bounced back and forth between the walls. "Nothing gets out of here … out of here … out of here … Won't get you anywhere … anywhere … anywhere …"

The Word put her hands over her ears, but the echoes grew louder. "To *Babel*... Babel... Babel... anywhere... anywhere... anywhere... out of here... out of here... out of here..." The echoes rained down on the Word from every side. "Meaningless words... words... words... To Babel... Babel... Babel... Meaningless... meaningless... meaningless..."

The Word couldn't bear it any longer. She hammered her fists on the walls, her eyes still shut tight. "Let me out!" she cried.

"Won't get you anywhere... anywhere... anywhere..."

"Stop! Please! Stop!" She opened her eyes and stared into the whiteness; she was so dazzled by its bright glare that she fell straight to the ground.

"Meaningless... meaningless... meaningless..." the echoes droned on.

She lay on the ground, utterly exhausted, her head pounding, until eventually her body surrendered and she fell into a comatose sleep.

When the brackets finally came to a standstill, the night had disappeared. But strangely, the night wasn't the only thing absent from the place where they had stopped. There was no day either – in fact, there was nothing at all that could be understood. There were no trees, no sky, not even any ground to stand on. The place made no sense, and yet the brackets had reached it. They let go of each other's hands. The word fell out onto the ground that didn't exist. Slowly, she opened her eyes. The whiteness was gone, she wasn't dazzled anymore. She could see – but she couldn't comprehend what she saw.

"Your new home. Babel, the rubbish dump of our world. Do you smell that?" The Word couldn't smell anything at all. "It stinks of nothing. A place full of meaningless words. The world doesn't need you."

"Shut up!" cried the Word. "I have a meaning!"

"Did you really think Song could give you meaning? What do *you* have to do with Song? You lost your meaning a long time ago."

With these wordlets the brackets disappeared, leaving the Word alone. She sat on the non-existent ground and cried tears that didn't exist. What if the brackets were right? Then a new fear dawned on her. She cast her eyes around this place that the brackets had called Babel, but she saw no place. And she saw no words. She realised there was not a single word around her that she understood.

CHAPTER
TEN

Babel

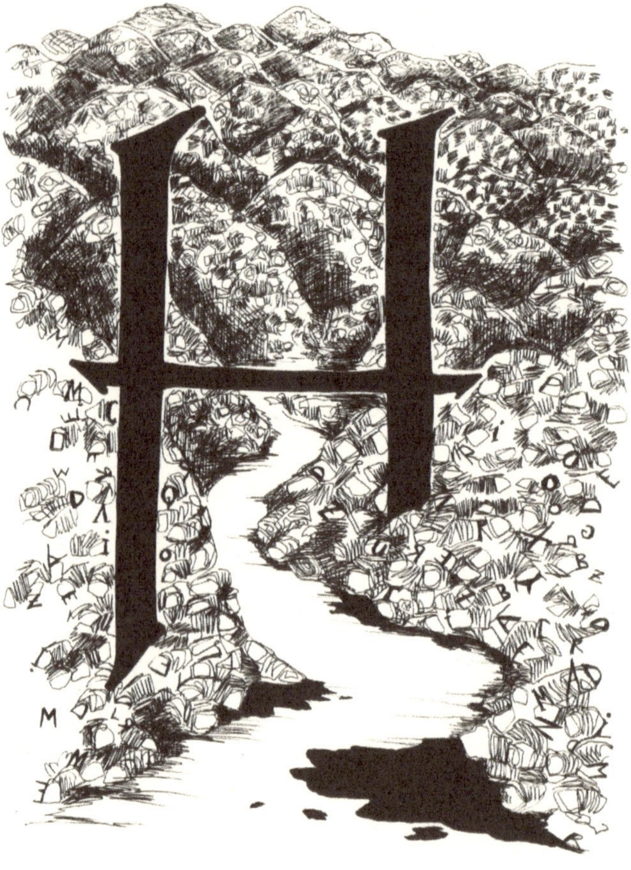

Hree I ma, igneekp ym sepormi. I swa yntwet seary dol henw I dame teh sepormi ot triew siht kobo... *Concentrate!*... Ti swa vwelte seary forbee I ftel the troys swa poemclet... *Concentrate!*... Onw ti smut nedf rof slitef. I illw ont gechan a drow fo ti onw, ron illw I dda a drow ot ti... *Wake up!*... Kanth ouy, read troys.

Tehn sdudelny she unedrsotod. The wrods aruond her wree still defroemd, but now she colud slolwy geuss thier maenigns. A breif mmoent of calrtiy fololewd by inocmperhnesoin ocne mroe. *Concentrate!* The wrodltes silpepd trhoguh her fignres. She ddin't wnat to thnik, she wnated to lie dwon and not eixst. She had no feleings – no sororw, no hpapinses, no desries, not a sinlge apsirtaion. She was no logner sekenig anytihng. She staerd nubmly inwrads, at her own lfielses slef. Notihng moevd. Tehre was no maennig. Notihng had eevr mdae or wuold eevr mkae sesne.

Concentrate!

The wrodlet flcikeerd bfeore her eeys. She treid to look depeer insdie herslef, braeknig trhuogh the hree and now and, for a mmoent, saw her own stroy. She saw a brid giudnig wrods wtih its wnigbaets. She was dnacnig wtih the otehr wodrs and was hpapy, she wanetd to saty tehre. Tihs cuold hvae been the end. She lay wtih the wodrs in the maeodw. Her eeys wree colsed, and wnated to selep ...

Concentrate! The wrodlet reapapeerd. Snog gaezd at her wtih his blcak eeys. Evrey wrod concaels a traesrue wtihin itslef, he had siad. Tehn the brakctes apepared befroe her. Did you ralely thnik Snog cuold gvie you macnnig? The pciture cahnegd. Now she was stnading in tornt of an unwroked blcok of stnoe in a gadren flul of sttaues. Ryhme and Raeosn wree tehre. The secnod stnoe smybolsies the end, Ryhme had siad. But nobdoy knwos yet how yuor sotry wlil end. Tehy btoh waevd fraewlel. The Wrod lokoed depeer stlil. She was stnading on the waetrsihp. She had lfet Mad and the haers behnid. Fraewlels, so mnay fraewlels. She saw Lokonig-Glsas. *Concentrate!* And for a mmoent, evreythnig was claer. She saw a huose biult in the shpae of a book, and her praents wvaing to her. The mmoent pasesd. Thcik fog semeed to flil her mnid agian, obsucrnig the mmeory whcih maent so mcuh to her, and whcih contanied wtihin it the maennig she had lsot. Her tsak was to saecrh for taht maennig – she was srue of it now.

The images that had been flashing before her eyes disappeared. She was in Babel, and although she could understand the words around her now, they were all completely out of context. The words were dotted about the place at random, unconnected, failing to form a clear picture.

That was close – the phrase flickered in her mind.

"W...?" the Word began, but then a series of wordlets appeared again.

Ahhh! Shhshhhshhhhhhhhhhhhh! You must not speak! Be careful!

The Word was silent.

You know you're in Babel. But what do you know about Babel? The brackets probably told you that Babel is the world's rubbish dump. Thousands of meaningless words. Uhhhaaa. They didn't tell you the whole story.

The Word listened carefully to the voice which spoke without making a sound, existing only inside her own head.

Babel isn't just a place, Babel is also a word. A meaningless word, until now, just as all words in Babel have been meaningless until now. But that's about to change. You are changing it.

"M...?"

Words only acquire meaning when they are part of a story. A solitary word without a story is meaningless. The story can be very short – sometimes a single sentence is enough – or it can be as long as a book. The most important thing is that humans find the right words to tell the story. If the storyteller is successful, the words in the story become meaningful. Babel is home to all the words whose stories are no longer told or who, like you, no longer remember their own story. Without a story, a word exists in isolation and ceases to make sense.

She listened to the wordlets and resisted the urge to ask all the questions that were buzzing around her head.

But what about Babel itself? Babel is in Babel, which should mean that its own story has been forgotten. But it hasn't been! We're telling it right now. A contradiction in terms? No! For Babel is part of your story, and your story is being told as we speak.

That's where we wordlets come in. We allow words to tell each other about the adventures they are sent on by humans. Whenever a word tells another word its story, it tells that story using us. In the beginning was the Word, that's true, but also the wordlets. We know every story, every adventure that any one of you has ever been on. But we also know that we have never been part of a story ourselves. Thus Babel became our home, too. We live here. A place of forgotten stories but also of stories that have never been told. Until today. Because we are part of your story, and in your story, we tell you all about Babel. We explain that this place is not as meaningless as it seems. Do you see it yet?

"W...?" she was about to ask, but the wordlets were already replying: *Babel*.

The Word looked around, and now she began to understand. The words that had previously been standing around the room at random were forming a pattern. The picture grew clearer, falling into place before her eyes like a mosaic. And then, for the first time, she could see where she was.

The sky above her was full of glowing clouds. The Word was standing on the brown earth of a path that wound its way between heaps of rubbish. Here and there, oily puddles had formed, streaked with colourful trails like melting rainbows. It was cold. The mingled odours of rubbish, rot and burning lay like a greenish-brown film over the landscape.

Go on, ask him.

The Word didn't understand.

"W...?"

Ask the word! Ask Babel.

"W...?"

Ask him what role he plays in your story.

"B...?"

Louder!

"B...?"

LOUDER!

Standing in Babel, surrounded by rubbish heaps, the Word cried: "Baaaabel! Baaaabel!" Her voice echoed over the hills.

The earth started to tremble beneath her feet. The Word fell to the ground. The rubbish heaps shifted, melted into each other. Two grey holes opened up in the thing before her, and stared at the very spot where she was lying. With a loud groaning sound, a mouth appeared below the two eyeholes and asked, "What do you want?"

The ground was still quaking. The Word struggled to her feet.

"The wordlets said you have a story to tell?"

Avalanches of rubbish tumbled down the mountain and were absorbed by the creature.

"No!" Babel replied.

No?

"Why not?" asked the Word.

"After all this time, I have absorbed thousands of words. All their stories have been forgotten. Now, at last, *I* am part of a story. At this very moment."

"Tell it to me, Babel. Tell me the story," pleaded the Word.

"If I tell it to you now, my story will eventually be forgotten too. Just like those of all the other words."

It's not just your story anymore, it's our story too! We all have a small part in it. All any of us can do is take on the role we are given within the story, and hope that if it is properly told, it will not be forgotten.

"Hope? Is that all?" asked Babel.

There is nothing else left to us.

The face that had formed in the gigantic rubbish-heap softened a little. Babel nodded, saying, "Very well." Then he began.

"Once upon a time, in a land beyond the limits of our imagination, there was a word called Babel. The land was called Babel too. There were no laws, no rules and no order. Quite simply, it was a place that nobody could understand. Like all other places, Babel consisted of words, but the words did not come together to form a picture. They were all jumbled up, and caused chaos. So Babel remained an incomprehensible place where language lay fallow, and would probably never have been of interest to anyone if a human hadn't taken up residence there. In the midst of the chaos, this human had built a hut. He sat at his table, looking out of the window into the distance now and again, but the quill in his hand never stopped moving. In the confusion of Babel, surrounded by thousands of words who had not been part of any story for a very long time, this human wrote a story.

It centred on a young word who thought she had lost her meaning. She embarked on a long journey, over the course of which she learned to understand her world. But she failed to find her meaning. Finally, she reached Babel, which to her seemed to be the most meaningless place of all. She was mistaken, however. As she began to understand Babel, she realised that her own story had originated there. Babel's story was not Babel's story, it was her story, their mutual story. Babel showed her the hut in which the human was writing their story. The word knocked on the ..."

Babel has fulfilled its role, just as we have fulfilled ours. Your story is not over yet. We don't know how it will end. No word has ever told it to another before. Don't be afraid of the ending. The road that takes you there is what matters. The ending itself is not the most important part. And don't forget: in the future, whenever you tell a word your story, wait for the right wordlets to come to you. Don't force us. When you say the right thing at the right time, it's like magic.

Hadn't Song said something similar about humans? The earth quaked, and Babel collapsed. The rubbish heaps moved apart, leaving a narrow path between them. It still stank, but the Word didn't even notice. The path led towards an open patch of ground where a wooden hut stood.

Now the Word knew what she had to do. In Babel's story, the word knocked on the door. She knew that word was her. If Babel had been telling the truth, she would find a human in the hut writing her story. It was a strange thought.

Her legs trembled as she walked towards the hut. She stopped outside the door and listened. She could hear a scratching noise coming from inside. The Word took a deep breath, raised her hand and knocked on the wood.

No answer.

Slowly, she pushed the door open. The room that lay before her was dimly lit. A single candle stood on the tabletop. At the table sat a man with his back to her.

"Hello," she said.

The man didn't turn around. The only sound was the continual scratching noise.

"When you're writing," said the man, "it's best to leave the world outside. Please be so kind as to close the door behind you when you come in. And take a seat. There's a chair here at the table for you."

The Word closed the door. After a few seconds her eyes grew accustomed to the faint glow from the candle, which was sufficient to illuminate the inside of the hut. On the shelves above the little bed stood row upon row of thick books. Perched on top of a chest on the other side of the room was a chessboard, its pieces skilfully crafted from pewter and so enchanting that they might have been plucked straight out of a fairy tale. *I wonder who he plays with?* she thought. There were lots of little slips of paper pinned to the walls, covered with scribbled notes in illegible handwriting.

The Word went over to the table and saw that the man was holding a white quill. Beside him stood an inkpot. He was scratching away diligently on a piece of paper. Her eyes fell on a bronze plaque near the table, with wordlets clearly engraved upon it:

> *For in the end,*
> *all we are doing is seeking*
> *to weave poetry into life,*
> *to find poetry in life itself.*

"Come and sit with me, then I can look at you while I write."

The Word sat down on the chair across the table from the man. She could see him clearly now. The light of the candle fell on his face. His hair was grey, his beard almost white. The frame of his glasses was so delicate it was almost invisible. His eyes were still fixed on his piece of paper, watching every movement of the quill.

"I've travelled alongside you for such a long time now, yet still I hardly dare raise my head to look at you," he said – but now he did look up. The quill still danced in his hand as his gaze rested on the Word's face.

"We're on page 147 of your story. I've had plenty of time to think about what I'd say to you once I had you here in front of me. But now that the moment has arrived, I still don't know."

The Word looked at the pile of papers on the table.

"Is it true? You've written my story?" she asked, sitting stock-still.

"Yes," he replied, and fell silent.

For a moment neither of them spoke, as they listened to the scratching of the quill.

"Is that it?" asked the Word, pointing to the pile of papers.

The man nodded. "Yes, that's it," he said. Then he paused and added, when he realised the Word wasn't going to say anything, "I've tried to get it across to you gradually, but it still feels rushed to me. I'm sorry."

The Word didn't understand. She racked her brains for the right questions to ask.

"But why? Why did you do all this?" she asked, feeling somewhat helpless.

"That's exactly why you're here. The whys and wherefores. You know a lot about your world by now, but the question remains: Why? What is your meaning, what is this whole story *for*?"

The Word nodded. "Why?" she asked.

The quill in the old man's hand seemed to be slowing. He was having difficulty with every wordlet he wrote.

"It was a long time ago that I discovered your world. It wasn't even a world so much as the idea of one. I didn't know how to tackle it. Your world was crammed full of words. Nothing moved. I sensed the stories hidden within it, but they were out of my reach. I needed a place untouched by chaos. A place of peace. I created this hut in the middle of this fallow field of language. I called the land around me Babel. A land full of rubbish, full of senselessly discarded words. I closed the door behind me and concentrated only on this place. I wanted to bring order to this newly discovered world, to unearth its hidden treasures, to find stories."

She gazed at the man's face. He was staring at the sheet of paper again. His eyes followed the quill in his hand. He's writing what he's saying, she thought. All this is part of the story.

"I created the brackets," he said. "Their task was to separate useful words from useless ones."

"You wanted to get rid of meaningless words," the Word broke in.

"Back then, I didn't know which words carried meaning and which ones didn't. I was just trying to spot patterns somewhere amongst the chaos. The brackets served me well. I began to see more and more clearly the outlines of a world that had nothing to do with Babel, a world full of life and movement. It was your world, the world as you know it – the world of language. But there was still something missing. Explaining a world is not the same thing as experiencing it. I had to allow others to enter your world: only then could it continue to exist. I needed a story.

One morning I was standing here in this room, looking at all the notes I'd made. I sat down at my table and looked out over Babel, over this vast kingdom full of possibilities, and I saw you there. I took up the first sheet of paper and started writing."

"You wrote me."

"Yes, I wrote about you and your parents. You argued

with your father. You didn't want to believe how important humans are to words. It worked! You were exactly the word I'd been looking for. I wanted to tell your story. But before I could send you off on your travels, you had to meet a human. He would make you forget your world, so that you could discover it all over again through fresh eyes. And with every detail you rediscovered, you would open up your world to somebody else."

The Word couldn't remember. She had argued with her father, she thought. She had parents.

"How could you do that to me?"

"I'm sorry for everything you've been through. I hope you can forgive me, once I've finished telling you the story."

"Finish it, then."

"I had to find a way to keep your world alive. Every word I wrote was a battle. It had to be right, to fulfil the specific task assigned to it. You can't write a story any way you like. The story decides. If you deviate from it, you get tangled up in lies that not a single soul believes. I couldn't risk that. Your story had to feel real. Because it was, it is. If it didn't feel right, nobody but me would ever get to know you. The world of language would sink back into Babel, forgotten forever."

The Word didn't understand. "Why?"

The man turned his gaze to the Word. "I'll show you. Look at the ink," he said, pointing to the inkpot on his right.

The Word looked at it.

"Are you ready?"

"Yes."

"Are you still looking?" he asked.

The Word was still looking at the same spot. The inkpot had disappeared. It was now standing on the other side of the table, to the man's left. His quill was busily scribbling away.

"How did you do that?" she asked.

The quill went on scratching.

"When you write, you shut out the world. If you close the door and concentrate, you can create a new world. Every word you write adds a new detail to this world. But if you stop writing, the world stands still; nothing moves, nothing speaks. Sad, isn't it?"

"What's that got to do with the inkpot?"

"During the brief moment in which I took hold of the inkpot, dipped my quill in it and moved the pot to the other side of the table, I stopped writing. Your world stood still, and you knew nothing about it. If I were to lay down my quill forever, you would cease to exist and not even realise it."

The Word hesitated. "The whole world can't just stop existing," she said, but she realised herself how empty her wordlets sounded.

"Why couldn't you have taken the most direct route to get here? Why couldn't I just have explained the whole world to you? The secret is not in discovering a world. The secret is in keeping it alive long after the last word has been written. If you'd come straight here by the most direct route, you would have marched straight into Babel, knocked on the door and asked, 'What's all this about the world of language?' Who would have bothered reading that? Who would have believed it? The readers are here with us. They are reading every line as we speak."

The Word looked at the quill, which was now moving very gently across the paper. "Who are they?"

"Humans. They are the ones you came on this journey for. You had to discover your own world so that they could discover it too. Only in that way could they take it to their heart. Now they can imagine your world. They know what the biscuits in the beech forest clearing taste like, and what the streets of the city of Langwich smell like. They've been to the Linguistic Games and felt on their faces the warmth of a thousand burning candles. And they know what it sounds like when a little bird sings. If they were to read to the end, they could use their imagination to create new pictures, and fill in the blank spaces in the mosaic which this book has left in their minds. Through them, our world could come to life again – even though I stopped writing your story a long time ago. And perhaps they won't forget our story."

"And now?" asked the Word.

"Now we can only hope."

The Word hesitated. The quill in the man's hand was moving more and more slowly.

"What if they forget?" she asked falteringly.

"Then it's all been for nothing."

The Word looked at him. "Is that it?" she asked. "Is that the end of the story?"

"No," he replied. "The readers are still waiting for something."

"For what?" she asked.

"I believe they want to know your name."

The Word smiled. "Me too. Will you share it with us?"

"Of course. But first, allow me to make things a little bit more exciting."

CHAPTER
ELEVEN

At the End

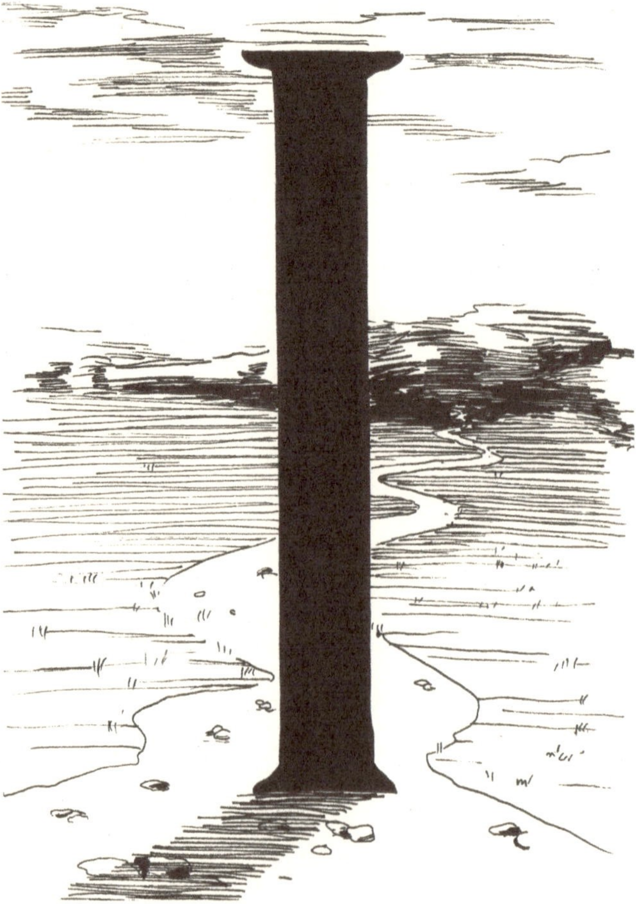
I

It was evening. A full moon was already visible in the sky, suffusing the darkness with a pale blue light. The crickets were chirping. The Word stood in a garden full of statues and heard the sound of hammering on metal, followed by snatches of song:

> *"We too are chipped away by time,*
> *The hours must pass, the clock must chime,*
> *I seize the moments, hold them fast,*
> *And yet I know: this too shall pass."*

It was Rhyme's voice. She was reciting the same poem the Word had heard her recite long ago. The Word followed her voice and made her way through the rows of statues.

> *"In the end the book is shut*
> *And we are left with nothing but*
> *Empty silence, blank and still*
> *No here, no now, no we, no will."*

The Word stood behind the sculpture of a kneeling man, holding his lover's hand. This was the sculpture Reason had used to propose to Rhyme, the Word recalled, and stepped out from behind the stone.

> *"We still feel the magic of the story*
> *Sense the words it brought to glory*
> *In dreams we fill the mosaic*
> *Escape the world so prosaic."*

Rhyme was perched on the little wooden bench, watching

her husband work. He was kneeling in front of the brass plaque at the foot of a block of stone, holding his hammer and chisel.

"It's late. Finish it tomorrow. You can't see properly in this light," said Rhyme.

"I'm almost done," Reason replied, and went on hammering at the sharp chisel.

Now Rhyme caught sight of the Word and beckoned her to sit beside her. "He is finishing your sculpture," said Rhyme.

The Word looked at the sculpture. The first stone symbolised the beginning of her story. It was unaltered, and showed a table with three words sitting around it. Her parents and her, thought the Word. She'd argued with her father, the man in the hut had said. What was new was the second stone, symbolising the end of her story. It showed a mother and father embracing their child. Tears brimmed in the Word's eyes as she looked at it.

"Go to him," said Rhyme, "go and see what's written on the brass plaque."

The Word stood up and went over to stand behind the kneeling Reason, who had now put aside his hammer and chisel.

"Finished," he declared.

Alone in the sky, the moon shone like a silent reader, following every wordlet of their conversation.

At the foot of the statue, the plaque read:

There was silence. Nothing moved. The old man sat in Babel. He dipped his quill into the inkpot, paused for a moment, and wrote:

Journey's End.

EPILOGUE

The old man set down his quill beside the inkpot. He picked up the pile of papers, and carefully squared them off until all the sheets lay stacked neatly on top of each other. Then he put the pile down, stood up and went to the door. One last time he turned back to the table and looked at the notes pinned to the walls. At that moment the candle went out, and he knew it was time to go. He opened the door and left the hut.

The End.

Elias Vorpahl | Author

Author's Afterword

When I wrote the story of "The Word Trove", I was also on a journey myself. I hope that you, dear reader, have been able to experience some of the excitement I felt while writing it.

This book has been over ten years in the making, so there are several people I would like to thank for their help in turning this story into a novel. Annemarie Albrecht from GGP Media GmbH, who tirelessly sent me new paper samples until the colour and the feel of the pages was just right. Lena Toschka, whose cover design and typesetting has lent the book its distinctive character. James Dawber, who showed me that a distance of over 18 000 kilometres need not be an obstacle to friendship, and who enriched the book with his suggestions about the English translation. My deepest gratitude to Julia Stolba: your illustrations have helped bring this world of words alive. Finally, since my wife has the last word about everything I write, I thank you, Diana, for your support, for your good taste and for your love.

I hope, dear reader, that even after some time – when you have placed this book on your bookshelf and moved on to others – you will still occasionally pick it up, leaf through the illustrations, and use your imagination to return to the world which you now have to leave behind. I thank you for your trust, and the interest you have shown in this story about something so very modest: a word.

Julia Stolba | Illustrator

Lena Toschka | Designer

Julia Marie Stolba, studied art history and visual arts in Munich and Kassel. Since 2014 she has worked as a freelance artist and illustrator. In her work she engages with the philosophical and socio-political issues of our time. Painting is her main form of artistic expression, and she works primarily with oil paints and watercolours, as well as chalk, charcoal and ink. Her pictures have been displayed at solo and group exhibitions in Germany and Austria.
"The Word Trove" is the first novel she has illustrated.

www.juliart.de

••••••••••●••••••••

Lena Toschka, née Stadler, works as a freelance graphic designer, illustrator and photographer under the name 'black to wild'. Following her studies in Halle (Saale) and Paris, she currently works in Berlin and Leipzig. She is passionate about craftsmanship, traditional illustrations and haptic experiences. Her visual language shows a love of detail and a variety of expressive techniques while remaining sensitive to the essentials.
"The Word Trove" is the first novel she has designed.

www.blacktowild.com

Romy Fursland | Translator

Translator's Afterword

Translating "The Word Trove" was an eye-opening process which threw up some unusual creative challenges. The way the book plays with words and explores the possibilities of language is one of its defining qualities, so it was vital to make sure that I retained it in translation. In some instances the plot of the story is dictated by wordplay, meaning that some parts of the book have had to be substantially rewritten to make them work in English. Translating wordplay can be a difficult task, but one that I have always considered one of the most enjoyable aspects of being a translator. This is translation at its most creative and its most fun. It reminds you of the endless possibilities of language – both the language you are translating from and the language you are translating into. It is also evidence of the heartening idea that everything is translatable, in one form or another, even if you have to depart quite radically from the original text to make it so.

The concept of dynamic equivalence (a term coined by linguist Eugene Nida) is an important one for translators. When you strive for dynamic equivalence, you are aiming to give readers of your translation the same experience as readers of the original text. Readers of the translation should be amused, surprised, moved, puzzled and delighted in the same way as readers of the book in its original language. This means that the translator has to recreate the effect the story has on the reader, rather than simply transposing what the text actually 'says' from one language to another.

In "The Word Trove", for example, various characters had to be renamed or completely reinvented in translation. Rhyme and Reason are 'Dichterin & Denker' ('Poet & Thinker') in the German text, and the hares were originally one character: a donkey ('Esel') who rearranged himself later in the story to become a different word ('lese', from the German for 'to read').

Inventing new puns was also great fun – the city of 'Langwich' and the 'Linguistic Games' are my attempts to recreate wordplay where it is found in the original text. Another strategy I used was including new wordplay in the translation where English offered the opportunity of doing so, in order to make up for the German wordplay 'lost in translation' elsewhere. The aim was to give readers of the translation the same overall experience as readers of the German text, and to retain the overarching effect of the book's playful use of language, even if certain individual instances of wordplay could not be directly translated.

I hope I have been successful in my attempt, and that you have enjoyed reading this translation. I have tried to make the magic of the world of language shine through these pages, and to make this exploration of the way language works (and plays) as enchanting in English as it is in German.

A WORD REARRANGES ITSELF

HARES
HUSH
SHARES
HUSH
SHARES
SH
SHARES
AR
S
SHARE
SHARE
SHARE

CONTENT

	PROLOGUE	9
ONE	SPEECHLESSNESS	13
TWO	BEGINNING AND END	25
TREE	A MAD TEA PARTY	39
FOUR	WATERSHIP DOWN	55
FIVE	IN THE TORRENT OF WORDS	65
SIX	LANGWICH	77
SEVEN	THE LINGUISTIC GAMES	91
EIGHT	THE WORD JOINS IN	113
NINE	A WINGED WORD	123
TEN	BABEL	139
ELEVEN	AT THE END	155
	EPILOGUE	161
	AUTHOR'S AFTERWORD	163
	CONTRIBUTORS	165